11.10

ACCOUNTING GOES PUBLIC

ACCOUNTING GOES PUBLIC

Morton Levy

UNIVERSITY OF PENNSYLVANIA PRESS / 1977

Library of Congress Cataloging in Publication Data

Levy, Morton, 1930–
     Accounting goes public.

     Includes index.
     1.   Accounting–Social aspects.   I.   Title.
HF5657.L428   657   77–81445
ISBN 0–8122–7733–3

Printed in the United States of America
Composition by Deputy Crown, Inc.

Contents

Acknowledgments   vii

Introduction   ix

Part One: Background and Beginnings

1. The Public Interest   3
2. Accounting Follows the Lead   11
3. API Organizes   23

Part Two: Getting Down to Cases

4. The Hill-Burton Act   43
5. Care for Dependent and Neglected Children   53
6. Political Campaign Controls   61
7. The Expansion of San Francisco International Airport   71
8. Financial Analysis of a Community College District   86
9. An Open Space Issue   107
10. Public Power   123

Part Three: A Look at the Future

11. Opportunities for Public Interest Accounting   147

Index   159

MW

2-6-78

Acknowledgments

The inadequacy of the English language, or at least my own facility with it, is exemplified by the traditional heading of this section of the book. "Acknowledgments" is more than inadequate, however; it is cold, impersonal and inaccurate. Therefore:

Thank You

To Eli Evans, then of the Carnegie Corporation of New York whose idea for a book about our experiences prompted me to write it. Eli later fought hard and successfully for a grant to the National Association of Accountants for the Public Interest which enabled me to spend the necessary time on the project.

To Professors Maurice Moonitz (University of California—Berkeley) and William Beaver (Stanford University) for their invaluable editorial assistance. Both then served on the board of directors of San Francisco Accountants for the Public Interest and willingly took time from their incredibly busy schedules to critique the first draft of every chapter of the manuscript.

To three students, Tom Doub, Warren Wicke and Henry Stachura who performed valuable research services for me and utilized their work for reports which partially fulfilled their requirements for M.B.A. degrees. Tom attended the University of San Francisco and worked on his report under Professor David Weiner, who was also an API director and who gave me much needed help on the early chapters. Warren and Henry were graduate students at the University of California at Berkeley where they were fortunate enough to have Professor Moonitz as their faculty advisor.

To Avery Russell of the Carnegie Corporation who encouraged me when I most needed it—and who taught me a few things about editors and publishers!

To Bob Erwin of the University of Pennsylvania Press, who wrote me when the manuscript was two-thirds completed to compliment us on our fine organization which he had just heard about. He casually (I think) observed, in the final paragraph, that I might someday wish to write a book about our experiences, and expressed his interest in publishing it. I answered promptly!

To my father-in-law, Joseph Fischer, who casually (I know) suggested the title for the book one day over dinner, which concluded months of fruitless searching for something which rang a bell for both Bob Erwin and me.

To Joe's daughter, Barbara Levy, for having so much patience with an impatient husband. Her quiet and calm nature encouraged and nurtured me—and still does. The word games she so often played with our three children resulted in a surprising resource for the book. When I searched for a key word, I usually found it from her. She also was magnificent in her assistance with proofreading the galleys and page proofs at a time when I barely could stand to look at the material again.

To all of the volunteers and staff at San Francisco API and all other APIs, without whose commitment and enthusiasm there would have been no story to tell.

With all of this gracious help, I feel somewhat reluctant to accept the title "author." But someone must accept the responsibility for errors and omissions.

Introduction

" 'Accountants for the Public Interest'? Why that's a contradiction in terms!" the foundation executive said with a chuckle, when I introduced myself as executive director of San Francisco Accountants for the Public Interest.

Since accountants, as a group, are not noted for a sense of humor, many of them probably would take serious exception to that comment, even though they might reluctantly admit that his sentiment is all too common. The American Institute of CPAs has issued this definition:

Accounting is a discipline which provides financial and other information essential to the official conduct and evaluation of the activities of any organization . . . It includes the development and analysis of data, the testing of their validity and relevance, and the interpretation and communication of the resulting information to intended users.[1]

What could be more in the public interest? Without the confidence of the financial community in the integrity of our reports it is not farfetched to say that our economic system would collapse.

Yet the reader can easily imagine the retort of those who have found accountants notorious for serving only big corporations and wealthy individuals: "What have you done for the 'public' part of 'public interest'—the masses who need your talents but can't afford their price tag? That's the kind of 'public interest' we're talking about these days."

The "public interest" movement of the past decade paralleled the civil rights movement of the early sixties and the growth of environmental and consumer organizations. This book will attempt to tell the story of the efforts by the accounting profession to follow and improve upon the path pioneered by the legal profession, the first to create a public interest structure within their formal organizations. It will describe the history, structure, program, and activities of the newer generation of professional public interest accounting organizations.

As of this writing, the first organization to establish and name itself

1. Statement issued by the Council of the American Institute of CPAs, 1967, *AICPA Fact Book*, May 8, 1975.

ix

Accountants for the Public Interest (API) is five years old. An umbrella organization, the National Association of Accountants for the Public Interest, (NAAPI) has been formed, with fifteen local affiliates spread throughout the country. This book is designed to serve as a manual for those in the accounting profession who wish to form new affiliates and to supply a model for those in other professions whose talents are desperately needed by groups involved in public interest activities. In so doing, it should also answer some of the questions accountants have about the motives and program of NAAPI. Finally, and most important, it may provide some insight for the "clients"—current and potential—of public interest accounting organizations.

Public interest accounting can serve various important needs for people unable to pay professional fees, including assistance for those individuals bedeviled by the complexities of their tax returns, helping small businesses cope with paperwork and forms required by government at all levels, or providing nonprofit community groups with adequate financial, management, or accounting talent. Although the following chapters will at least touch on these matters, most of the book will be devoted to services that may be best described as "issue-oriented."

Virtually every major public policy issue, from the local to the national level, has financial or accounting overtones. Oil pricing, mass transit, campaign spending, nuclear power, open space, utility regulations, medical malpractice insurance, school budgets, health services, no-fault insurance—all require a thorough understanding of the accounting data for the intelligent evaluation of alternative proposals.

Frequently, public policy controversies pit the public, traditionally unorganized and lacking in expertise, against industry or government, both well able to afford all the expertise money can buy. Government may have represented the public in the past, but few sophisticated analysts would argue that it does so today. Bureaucracy and inertia have bred their own biases, as governments themselves have lately begun to acknowledge by setting up public advocates, ombudsmen, and other means to support third-party interventions in policy disputes.

Furthermore, frequent controversies between and within levels of government call for some channel through which the public may receive explanations or reconciliation of opposing claims that are each apparently buttressed by reliable facts and figures.

Those who previously have had little or no representation in decision-making clearly need a voice. People no longer meekly accept "the facts"; they want to understand them. If Americans are to regain confidence in their political, social, and economic institutions, all sides of important public issues must be represented. All those who have information, talents, or expertise must find ways to make them available to those who cannot afford to pay.

This book opens with a brief history and discussion of the term "public interest." It then moves on to examine how the legal profession became involved in the movement to make available professional advice to those who could not afford to pay, with particular emphasis on institutionalization within the profession and the organized bar. Next is a review of the "pro bono publico" efforts of the accounting profession, and a description of some situations in which the "public" side of a controversy has suffered from the unavailability of technical accounting services. These instances dramatize the role accountants can and should play and their potential value because of the general acceptance of their independence.

The organization and development of the first API will be examined in some detail, with attention to professional and ethical problems such as independence, quality control, publicity, conflicts of interest, competition, and liability insurance.

Chapters four through ten offer a series of API case studies. Each chapter reviews the controversy and the engagement and contains pertinent portions of the report issued to the client, client evaluations, post-report developments, and conclusions concerning the implications of the case and the lessons and principles that can be drawn from it.

The final chapter examines possible future problems that public interest accounting will have to face. The need for support from the organized profession will be discussed along with the opportunities the movement offers to the profession. The need and prospects for developing sources of long-range funding are examined in depth. Finally, an attempt is made to analyze the potential of an interdisciplinary structure to deal with public policy questions in a less fragmented and more effective way than is now possible.

In short, this book seeks not only to inform the public about a new and promising movement in its behalf but also to inform more of those in the very profession whose members have mobilized that movement.

Institutional support from the profession itself for public interest accounting would contribute substantially to the growth and stability of the movement. Such support could be generated by outside pressure from government, internal pressure from younger members of the profession, the desire to emulate other professions, as well as the recognition that such action is consistent with its professional and social responsibilities and its own self-interest. When the leaders of the profession possess more vision, courage, and maturity, they will lend their support to the concept of public interest accounting. At that time, we will all have better answers for that foundation executive, and, of greater importance, the profession will be more effectively participating in the solution to some of our country's most pressing problems.

___(**Part One**)___

Background and Beginnings

_____

___(1)___

The Public Interest

Whether in fact there is a *public* interest distinguishable from the interests of individuals, groups, or classes has been a matter of debate in the Western tradition since Plato. In *The Republic,* Plato appealed to citizens to consider the "good of the whole" as necessary to a moral and just state. In his "happy state," "not the disproportionate happiness of any one class, but the greatest happiness of the whole" was the goal, and in this "state which is ordered with a view to the common good of the whole we should be most likely to find justice."[1]

Many other classical scholars and philosophers have used "public good," "common interest," and the like to characterize the concept now generally termed the "public interest." The work of Robert Ardrey eloquently demonstrates the historic subordination of individual rights to the "public interest" to secure survival of the various species within the animal kingdom. Early man faced the same dilemma between promotion of the "public interest" or extinction in his quest for sustenance and for protection from wild beasts and hazardous elements.

Even in modern times survival is a problem, but it appears in different forms. In our highly organized and specialized societies, individual and group interests still conflict, but equally vigorous disputes arise between one person's (or group's) rights and another's. No individual interest or right is absolute and final. None exists in a vacuum. The right to freedom of speech is among our most cherished national principles, but even *it* is balanced by the laws against slander.

Indeed, balance and cooperation seem to be the linchpins to understanding the current usage of the term "public interest," at least among those who consider themselves part of the movement of the past decade. This era has also generated vocal and deep-seated opposition which is symbolized by the dispute over the meaning, if not the ownership, of the term "public interest." Organizations claiming to represent the public interest are accused of arrogance, presumption, or worse, and their motives are suspect.

1. Plato, *The Dialogue of Plato,* trans. Benjamin Jowett, Britannica Great Books, vol. 7 (Chicago: Encyclopaedia Britannica, 1952), p. 342.

In our complex society, few important issues permit absolute precision in identifying *the* public interest once and for all. Two examples should suffice:

Reserving land for open space is clearly a public interest issue. Environmentalists represent a broad public that seeks uncrowded conditions, recreational facilities, and conservation of natural resources and wildlife. On the other hand, two other broad "publics" have a deep interest in the issue—the labor unions that seek more jobs, and people in search of housing. Each group constitutes a public whose interest may be in conflict with one of the other group's interests. Who can say which group, if any, truly represents the public interest?

Social welfare problems pose much the same dilemma. As a society, we have decided that food, clothing, shelter, health care, and other basic necessities of life must be provided to all. The taxpayers, however, who must foot the bill for the disadvantaged's needs have their own interests to protect. Where is *the* one and only public interest to be found in these examples?

No public interest organization or its supporters contend that it represents the only public interest. Their titles then should use "a" rather than "the," implying their own recognition—and encouraging the public's—of the multiplicity of interests. The "Center for Law in *a* Public Interest" or "Accountants for *One* of the Public Interests" sounds downright silly! Names, however, are simply outward symbols for the underlying substance. Public interest organizations need make no apologies for their names. Their deeds testify to their objectives and program.

Public interest means the representation of those who are generally ignored or overpowered in our society. By providing these people with technical assistance, public interest organizations lend some balance to the decision-making processes and thus validate and legitimize the choices ultimately made in matters of broad concern to the citizenry.

A comment once offered by Roscoe Pound well states the special responsibility of the service professions:

There is much more in a profession than a traditional dignified calling. The term refers to a group of men pursuing a learned art as a common calling in the spirit of public service—no less a public service because it may incidentally be a means of livelihood. Pursuit of the learned art in the spirit of a public service is the primary purpose.[2]

It is entirely appropriate that the service professions bear a heavy responsibility for public interest activities. Because they are licensed by

2. Roscoe Pound, *The Lawyer from Antiquity to Modern Times* (St. Paul, Minn.: West Publishing, 1953).

the state and given monopolistic privileges and protection they are deeply indebted for their success to the communities in which they function. Their talents are available for sale to those who can afford to pay for them. When others, who cannot afford to pay, need those same talents for the balanced consideration of broad public issues, considerations of justice and gratitude indicate that they should be provided.

If justice or gratitude are insufficient, a purely selfish reason can be added: the monetary rewards and influential positions that members of these professions enjoy would be severely threatened by a collapse of present institutions. These institutions rest on the support and confidence of the public. To deny that public the representation and input into those institutions that it is now demanding is to invite accelerating political and economic decay.

Doctors, lawyers, clergy, accountants, teachers, economists, engineers, scientists, and architects can have few, if any, more important goals than the investigation of public policy issues, the objective evaluation of the underlying assumptions, and the independent assessment of how well government is serving the public interest.

One Profession Takes the Lead

Ethical Consideration 2-25 of the Code of Professional Responsibility of the American Bar Association reads:

The basic responsibility for providing legal services for those unable to pay ultimately rests upon the individual lawyer . . . every lawyer, regardless of professional prominence or professional workload should find time to participate in serving the disadvantaged. The rendition of free legal services to those unable to pay reasonable fees continues to be an obligation of each lawyer, but the efforts of individual lawyers are often not enough to meet the needs.

The first organized efforts of the bar to implement this pronouncement resulted in the legal aid societies. Although legal aid was available in the United States as early as 1876, there were only forty-one formal organizations as late as 1916. The real growth in the movement began six years later, when the American Bar Association recommended that every state and local bar association appoint a standing committee on legal aid.

Generally, legal aid remained a charitable rather than a professional responsibility. Few lawyers participated in it, and most of them were on the staffs of the legal aid societies and regarded as marginal by the practicing bar. Lawyers did support the work financially, possibly on the theory that it would ease the pressure for free service required of them by the bar.

If an attorney in private practice wished to handle a legal aid case, his firm generally required that he do so on his own time. The subtle assumption was that pro bono work was not part of a lawyer's professional obligation, but an avocation.

This attitude was not universal, however. In a sharply critical passage, Reginald Heber Smith wrote:

In all their work, legal aid societies are relieving the Bar of a heavy burden by performing for the Bar its legal and ethical obligation to see that no one shall suffer injustices through inability because of poverty to obtain needed legal advice and assistance. Each case which a legal aid organization undertakes puts the Bar in debt to it for in the conduct of that case, it is doing the work of the Bar for the Bar.[3]

Single-purpose agencies such as the American Civil Liberties Union and the National Association for the Advancement of Colored People filled the increasingly apparent gap between the bar's canonical words and its deeds on behalf of the poor until the 1960s brought new attention to poverty and social injustice. Recognition of the limitations of legal aid voluntarism was forced on the bar in part by ever louder and more persistent demands for specific legal services and for broader legal and political access. One result was the central role the American Bar Association played in the decision to include a legal services component in the Office of Economic Opportunity (OEO).

The OEO, created in 1964, attempted to provide a vehicle through which organized professional attention might finally be paid to the broad delivery of free legal services to the poor. When the program participated in controversial cases and undertook efforts at law reform, the ABA actively defended it against its critics. The ABA's awakened realization also led to major revisions in its Code of Professional Responsibility, and reflected its recognition that legal services to the poor should be extended by the public sector of the profession even while the private bar became more fully involved through the legal aid model.

The OEO programs and lawyers helped underscore the major failure of the private bar to address policy issues. The OEO guidelines called for "funds . . . to implement efforts initiated . . . by local communities to provide the advice and advocacy of lawyers for people in poverty," an extension of the legal aid model. They also sought "empirical knowledge" and "experiment and innovation to find the most effective method to bring the aid of the law and the assistance of lawyers to the economically disadvantaged" and "to sponsor education and research in the areas of

3. Reginald Heber Smith, *Justice and the Poor* (New York: Carnegie Foundation), p. 243.

procedural and substantive law which affect the causes and problems of poverty."[4]

The guidelines reinforced the new consciousness in the bar itself by setting a goal of educating it to "its essential role in combating poverty." Furthermore, recognizing that the "poor do not always know when their problems are legal [ones]" and may be distrustful of the profession, the OEO aimed "to teach the poor and those who work with the poor to recognize problems which can be resolved best by the law and lawyers."[5]

The shift—or enlargement—of emphasis both arose from and generated new efforts of the bar itself. These efforts began to remove pro bono work from the realm of charity to that of professional duty.

According to an article in the *Yale Law Journal:*

The present day public interest lawyer feels that the old style pro bono work, while admirable, is no longer adequate to cope with the problems we face. Rather than devoting his energies to the defense of the constitutional rights of individuals, he feels that he must take more affirmative action and think in broader social, economic and political terms. He is committed ultimately to causes, not clients.[6]

The Public Interest Law Firm

In calling for support by the organized bar for public interest law firms, Chesterfield Smith confirmed this broadening of the concept of pro bono work:

While activity on behalf of the indigent is laudable and must continue, it is now apparent that this concern is only one part of the total obligation of the legal profession to ensure that each and every segment of society is adequately represented.[7]

Evidence of the rooting of the concept is the ABA's new section on public interest practice, which is fully staffed at its Chicago national headquarters, and the appropriation of $60,000 through the ABA's Fund for Public Education in support of the newly formed Council for Public Interest Law. (The Council is also financed in its first year by grants from the Ford Foundation, the Rockefeller Brothers Fund, and the Edna McConnell Clark Foundation.)

4. F. Raymond Marks, *The Lawyer, The Public, and Professional Responsibility* (Chicago: American Bar Foundation, 1972), p. 43.
5. Ibid.
6. 79 *Yale Law Journal,* 1146.
7. President's Page, *American Bar Association Journal,* 641 (1974).

> A central assumption of our democratic society is that the general interest or the common good will emerge out of the conflict of special interests. The public interest law firm seeks to improve this process by giving better representation to certain interests. As such, it is an American variation on the theme of the Ombudsman.[8]

Thus wrote Edward H. Levi, who was later to become Attorney General of the United States. According to some, the public interest law firm is the most significant development in the private sector of the legal profession. It has the potential of influencing the definition of professional responsibility to the public; and, because in so many of its cases the government has been the adversary, it shatters the myth that government lawyers represent the public. A few illustrations of the modern public interest law firm will demonstrate the scope of their activities.

Three years after the attempts of General Motors to discredit him had succeeded only in making him something of a public hero, Ralph Nader established the Center for Study of Responsive Law in 1969 in an effort to make corporations and regulatory agencies more responsive to consumer interests.

The Lawyers' Committee for Civil Rights Under Law, whose board of trustees includes senior partners from many of the nation's most prestigious law firms, a former U.S. Supreme Court Justice, twelve former top government officials and cabinet members, and eight former presidents of the American Bar Association, describes its overall philosophy eloquently: "The American promise is that we will MAKE THE SYSTEM WORK FOR EVERYONE. It is the high calling for lawyers to make certain that promise is kept, for unless the law can redress real grievances and serve as the instrument of reform, men will look elsewhere for relief."[9]

California Rural Legal Assistance has numerous offices throughout the rural parts of the state and a central office in San Francisco to coordinate major efforts involving law reform and class-action suits.

The Center for Law and Social Policy, in Washington, joins experienced lawyers with law students in a program of public interest representation in the federal context. It is concerned primarily with consumer affairs, environmental protection, and health, and has been especially active in cases relating to the constitutional rights of the mentally ill.

Business and Professional People for the Public Interest, in Chicago, has a full-time professional staff of lawyers and researchers and is supported by local business and professional people and foundations. It

8. Edward H. Levi, in a foreword to *The Public Interest Law Firm: New Voices For New Constituencies* (New York: Ford Foundation, 1973), pp. 7–8.
9. Marks, op. cit., pp. 128–9.

institutes action on behalf of the general public in such matters as safety and health, housing and discrimination, police procedures and public administration, favoritism in taxation, and conflict of interest in government.

Notwithstanding their organizational and functional diversity, these organizations maintain a common focus: "public duty . . . not ancillary to any other function . . . but a reason for their being."[10] Another striking similarity among them is the recognition that government—federal, state, or local; judicial, legislative, or administrative—is the adversary. Whether as friendly adversary or active enemy, government is the opponent in virtually every case or project of the public interest law firm. On its face, this may be startling. The affairs of the public, however, are supposed to be conducted through government. Because our government, while increasing in size and complexity, has also become increasingly remote, it has become the natural target of intermediary efforts on behalf of that public.

The Response of Private Law Firms

Private law firms have responded to the increasing pressure for support of public interest efforts in a variety of ways. Many larger established law firms have designated a public interest partner or committee. At a minimum, such designation acknowledges public responsibility as an appropriate subject for formal consideration, and focuses the attention of the firm's staff on matters that previously were not considered part of its business.

Some of these firms do not seem to identify public interest work as firm work. Other firms encourage the intake of public interest matters as an integral part of their work, frequently because they believe it is the firm's social responsibility. Still other firms have expanded the concept by establishing a public interest department. This approach manifests permanency and professionalization and institutionalizes the firm's responsibility to support pro bono efforts.

Whatever form the response has taken, a major breakthrough has plainly occurred. The establishment law firms no longer can be described as indifferent to the public interest movement. Some formal structures are being developed that recognize that lawyers, as lawyers, owe a duty to society at large, thus rejecting the traditional view that a lawyer's professional life is separable from his personal commitments and his social conscience.

10. Ibid., p. 152.

Conclusion

Although few would claim that the legal profession has done all it can or should do to fulfill its social responsibilities, even fewer would dispute that the profession's commitment and activities far outstrip those of any other profession. The lessons to be learned by other professions are well summarized by F. Raymond Marks:

The most striking thing about the new public interest lawyers is their belief that their skills and training do not disqualify them as active participants in community dialogue . . . Independent of their role as lawyers, they [feel] compelled to participate in the controversies of their time . . . to enlist their professional skills and involve their professional lives in their social concerns.

And all of us would do well to heed his further observation:

There is a new awareness on the part of the Bar that the country is in serious trouble and that we'd better begin working within our institutions to straighten things out. Right now![11]

11. Ibid., p. 215.

___(2)___

Accounting Follows the Lead

It is not surprising that, in seeking to develop a public interest structure, a group of accountants followed the legal model. Most accountants have close working relationships with lawyers and great respect for them. The prototype had proven to be workable and effective, and law was the only profession that offered a model!

Those who undertook this development viewed public interest accounting as a logical and timely extension of public interest law. The "pure" legal issues of civil rights, civil liberties, due process, and the like had been substantially dealt with by legal services organizations in the 1960s. American society now seemed to be entering an era of complex, multidimensional, and interdisciplinary problems. Balanced consideration of such issues as campaign financing and spending controls, utility regulations, health care costs, school financing, and prison reform call for contributions from all of the professions. Their financial components strongly suggest a prominent role for accountancy.

Initial Efforts

The concept of community service grew slowly in the accounting profession, especially service on an organized basis. Although it cannot be empirically established, probably the very first Certified Public Accountants (CPAs) who were licensed in New York in 1896 assisted those unable to pay. Since then, anecdotal evidence suggests that few practitioners have failed to follow their example, though there have been differences in the degree of involvement and variations in the type and focus of the services provided. During the profession's early years, most of the uncompensated services were probably clerical or bookkeeping. With the growth in stature of the profession, they have evolved to a far more sophisticated level, especially in the past generation.

Now CPAs frequently serve on governmental commissions, on the boards of schools, hospitals, and universities, or as treasurers for churches, political candidates, or the United Way. Although some bookkeeping

11

work is still being done, the charitable work now includes sophisticated management consulting and audits.

Many firms now bill for these services at their standard rates and then remit part or all of the fee received as a charitable donation. This procedure has several advantages. First, it clearly identifies the amount of the contribution and enables the firm to maintain its rate structure. Secondly, staff assigned are less likely to be psychologically penalized for working on "free" jobs. Lastly, the act of paying focuses the client's attention on the value and costs of the assignment, and it facilitates the phasing of the client from a "no-pay" to a "part-pay" basis, if and when this becomes desirable.

These community services activities have some common threads. First, they are all sponsored by an individual accountant or a firm. Secondly, they serve as the principal charitable activity for the individual accountant or firm. Thirdly, most of them are aimed at promoting business.

This kind of unorganized sponsorship severely limits the impact of the community services that accountants have performed. If someone in need does not know an interested or sympathetic CPA, he is out of luck. Any inquiries he makes are likely to be fruitless since those who do provide such service avoid publicity, preferring to choose their beneficiary clients quietly. Word spreads anyway, resulting in an unfair and unequal burden on some firms and individuals.

New Directions

Apart from these individual, isolated efforts, "pro bono publico" was conspicuously absent from the lexicon of the accounting profession until recently. This reflected the attitude that community service arose from an individual's (or at best, a firm's) decision for assisting a specific group or organization rather than from a professional or social responsibility to the community. Thus, efforts were aimed at the good of, say, the Boys' Club, and not at the public good in general. Moreover, the organized profession (represented largely by the American Institute of Certified Public Accountants) apparently felt little, if any, discomfort with this position. Social responsibility was a personal matter, and the leaders of the profession had no duty, beyond occasionally exhorting their colleagues "to become involved," to challenge this perception. The situation began to change in the late sixties. The riots of that period awakened the conscience of the American people—partly, no doubt, with the alarm of fear that the disturbances generated. Forced to comprehend the problems afflicting the black population and the potentially disastrous effects of continued failure to deal with them constructively, the leaders in our society responded with actions that ran the gamut from repression to legislative reforms.

Aid to Black Businesses

One of the more popular new programs, sponsored by the federal government and the private sector, sought to support black capitalism. The accounting profession's contribution, assistance to disadvantaged owners of small businesses, was the first organized effort within the profession toward a formal structure for pro bono work. Initiated by interested and committed individuals through state societies of Certified Public Accountants in Massachusetts, New York, Illinois, Missouri, and California, the program soon drew in more states; and the AICPA established a division to coordinate and service the state groups, which was funded for a time by the U. S. Office of Minority Business Enterprise (OMBE). The programs bear many different names but are similar in operation. Firms, and occasionally individual CPAs, are recruited as volunteers and local agencies are told of their availability. The volunteers are assigned to cases on a rotating basis and retain complete control and responsibility for the client. No fees are charged for the initial work, although the client may eventually pay part or full fees as his business improves. While some of the groups present seminars or training sessions for clients, most of their activity is on the usual, one-to-one client basis.

What is unusual for the highly trained and experienced CPA volunteer is the level of work encountered. He is likely to be involved in reconstructing records, general ledger postings, and bank reconciliations. Only rarely will he become associated with the client early enough to train him, or his personnel, in rudimentary bookkeeping and control procedures and to set up and supervise the accounting system. Far too often he is called in when a situation is beyond salvage. Therefore, he is frequently frustrated and dissatisfied with the results of his labors.

Almost all of these programs are further handicapped by the unwillingness or inability to get the message about the availability of the service to the black community. Newspaper publicity doesn't work, contact with civic leaders and banks has been ineffective, and mailings to minority organizations and church groups have produced only slight response. Complex factors underlie this state of affairs: (1) Many people in the black community don't know what a CPA is or what he does. (2) Many don't recognize or understand their own business needs. (3) The offices through which the services are brokered, usually those of the CPA society, are located in downtown high-rise buildings which are off the "turf" of the people in need.

Outreach poses a difficult sociological problem—one beyond the scope of this book. The problem has been thoroughly researched and is clearly solvable. As experience has taught, however, the solution does not lie in simply announcing, "Here we are to do our good work—come and get it!"

Many of the CPA organizations have effectively abandoned outreach by limiting their programs to clients screened by OMBE "call contractors." These government-funded entities package services for minority entrepreneurs, from loan applications to advice on legal, accounting, and marketing matters. Some observers have questioned the propriety of OMBE, which is itself funded to provide these services, contracting them out to private organizations that themselves seek volunteer services from CPAs and other professionals. Because this too is a complex issue involving multiple and sometimes conflicting goals and the uncertainties of any experiment, it also lies outside the scope of this book.

The threshold question is the effectiveness of the black capitalism program. Can you successfully put people into business, or keep them in business, by supporting them with dollars and technical assistance? Does it make more sense to build the foundation for long-term success by educating and training the culturally deprived so they might eventually have a reasonable chance to succeed in the highly competitive and speculative arena of American small business? The evidence is that the approach taken was little more than cosmetic and political, and has failed.

In June 1975, the U. S. Commission on Civil Rights issued a stinging report, charging that lethargy, incompetence, and bigotry have crippled federal programs to aid minority-owned businesses ever since the programs began in 1969.

A survey of programs sponsored by state CPA societies proved equally disheartening. Among the findings:

- Most had a greater supply of volunteers than of clients.
- The biggest single effort was expended in record reconstruction.
- Among the few societies that kept such statistics, the largest number of estimated total hours spent in the latest full year of activity was 350.
- Most clients did not request assistance in time to minimize their problems.
- Few societies were making vigorous efforts to attract clients to their programs.
- None has established evaluation criteria for its program.

The efforts by the formal CPA organizations have been no more successful than the sometimes duplicate programs sponsored by the National Alliance of Businessmen, the National Association of Accountants (composed mostly of those working in private industry), the Urban League, and others. In a massive misuse of talent, tens of thousands of hours have been spent by well-meaning and highly trained professionals to little effect. The most a CPA could do in this setting was, by reconstructing records and performing bookkeeping services, to enable a handful of black businessmen to remain in business a few months longer than they otherwise might. Nevertheless, though it failed woefully in its avowed purpose, the program had one major unexpected achievement: it raised the consciousness of many individuals to the needs of the community beyond their private practices, and to the role they might play in meeting them.

Tax Assistance Programs

Paralleling the program for disadvantaged businesspeople was an effort to assist individual taxpayers. In 1968, Professor Bernard Goodman, who was teaching a course in taxation at the University of Hartford, in Connecticut, proposed to his class of twenty-five an experimental program of assistance to taxpayers. To his own amazement, he recruited twenty-five eager volunteers. On the program's first night, the students had one client. Local residents were plainly skeptical about the services the group professed to offer. Four weeks went by before business picked up at all, and only in the final two weeks of the tax season was there substantial demand. In the first year, sixty-five taxpayers were assisted. Although Professor Goodman and his volunteers were disheartened by the apathetic response, they were convinced of the worthiness of the program, and persisted. Vindicating their faith, approximately 300 people availed themselves of the service in the following year.

In 1969 another tax assistance program was begun in Los Angeles by Philip Storrer and Gary Iskowitz, agents for the Internal Revenue Service, and a third in New York City by Jeffrey Gold, a Masters in Business Administration candidate at Baruch College, City University of New York. None of these three groups was aware of the others, but they displayed striking similarities.

Although Storrer, Iskowitz, and Gold are now CPAs, they, like Professor Goodman, were then outside the mainstream of the profession— none was a full-time practitioner. Likewise, all of them were concerned by the complexities presented to the average taxpayer by the revised tax forms for the tax year 1969, which came out in 1970. In the name of tax reform, people who had been getting the short form IBM card 1040A and a two-page instruction sheet now were receiving the complete and imposing form 1040 and a sixteen-page instruction booklet.

In forming Community Tax Aid, Inc. (CTA), Jeffrey Gold looked to local legal aid programs for guidance. The most important lesson was that the mere existence of such help does not assure its use. The poor find lawyers remote and, worse, dangerous. Even if the indigent person can be convinced that free legal help does not threaten him, he may wonder whether the man sitting in the broken chair behind the beat-up desk is competent. If so, why is he slumming?

Gold faced analogous problems in attempting to deliver tax assistance. To avoid remoteness, he chose a storefront location in a poverty neighborhood. To counteract any impression that CTA was merely bureaucracy in a new package, he refused free space in government office buildings. In its second year, CTA received a foundation grant which permitted opening two additional storefront locations. Operations ran from mid-February through April 15 at all three. Additional offices were opened in succeeding years, and some 2,300 taxpayers were served in 1974. Similar success was achieved by Storrer and Iskowitz in Los Angeles.

The organized profession has been slower to participate in this program than they were in that directed toward minority business. In a survey of all state CPA societies about such activities, only five responded and two of those indicated that their programs might be terminated due to inadequate client response. (No response was received from two other states known to be sponsoring such a program.) In one of the largest states, fifty professional volunteers spent 300 hours and were assisted by seventy-five students at six locations. They prepared just 250 tax returns in 1975, 200 less than the year before. Ten volunteers and thirty students in another state prepared thirty returns in 1975. The lack of enthusiasm is both a cause and an effect of the outreach problem. Any salesman who is not excited about his product will not sell much of it, and the inability to communicate with ghetto dwellers compounds the difficulties of the program and its supporters. As one state society respondent put it, "We were there but the low-income taxpayers didn't take advantage."

Besides the outreach problem, the CPA-sponsored taxpayer assistance program has encountered questions about its necessity and advisability, though each can be readily answered:

The Internal Revenue Service has extensive free programs of assistance, which should be sufficient. However, the IRS often is not accessible to the poor and its hours, which coincide with those of working people, are inconvenient. It does not prepare state or local returns. In addition, many of the poor regard the IRS as the enemy and unlikely to look out for their interests.

Commercial tax services can do the job inexpensively. They can, but do they? Some of them are notorious for overcharging, many are ill-trained when they are trained at all. The well-managed, reputable, and competent tax services frequently shun low-income neighborhoods.

CPA volunteers are needed during the tax season, the time of year when they are busiest with paying clients. This is true, but not all CPAs are heavily involved in tax work. Audit or management-services staff might be available along with those working for private industry.

The Accounting Aid Society

Against this background of well-meaning but faltering efforts, the Accounting Aid Society of Des Moines, Iowa, opened its doors in October 1969. Like the others, its program encompassed taxpayer assistance and aid to disadvantaged businesspeople, but it also included accounting assistance to nonprofit community groups and financial counseling to low-income individuals. Easily the most comprehensive and ambitious pro bono accounting effort attempted to that date, AAS was started by an accounting student, John C. Neubauer, who was then enrolled at Drake University in Des Moines. Neubauer explained his motivation in an article in the May 1971 issue of the *Journal of Accountancy*:

Individually, accountants have exhibited their social concern by participation in many civic, philanthropic and humanitarian activities. Unfortunately, as pointed out by Ralph W. Estes, "The traditional forms this participation has taken are not sufficient and are not directed toward the root causes of the more pressing problems of our society."

The program was also a response to the dilemma familiar to all university accounting students: the scarcity of opportunities to apply their newly acquired skills to real cases. Drake, like most schools where accounting programs are offered, can offer few opportunities for actual experience beyond bookkeeping for the corner grocer or a handful of internship openings.

Neubauer stressed the "internship" feature of the program in his appeal to the accounting faculty at Drake, as well as the clearer understanding of societal problems that participation in the program would provide. The response of the faculty was unanimously favorable. Many community leaders also lent their support and guidance on the dimensions and directions of the program. The Iowa CPA Society was an early supporter of AAS, providing leadership, volunteers to supervise the students, and substantial funding in the first year of operations. In that year, AAS assisted 25 small businesses, 15 nonprofit organizations, and 150 individuals in the low-income community. AAS received an OEO grant of $77,000 to provide assistance in professional money management and consumer affairs to the poor in the year beginning July 1,

1970. In mid-1971 after the appearance of Neubauer's article in the *Journal of Accountancy* had generated many inquiries, AAS applied for a much larger grant to support the national expansion of the program. Notwithstanding initial enthusiasm for it by OEO officials, the grant application was rejected due to the cutbacks in federal funding for the poverty program.

In another serious setback, the Iowa society withdrew its support, apparently because it disapproved of AAS's link with a consumer activist organization. In 1972, Neubauer resigned as executive director and moved out of the state. AAS activities diminished and in 1973 the program in Des Moines was abandoned (though it was reorganized in 1975 under a new name, Business Aid Society).

The program did not die without heirs, however. It fathered four other AASs, still in operation in 1976. The organizations in Charlotte (North Carolina), Detroit, Hartford, and Minneapolis differ from one another and from the original Des Moines group in their emphasis on specific programs, probably in reflection of the differing priorities of their leaders. The Detroit program, which at the outset resembled the one in Des Moines, now is primarily concerned with assistance to nonprofit organizations. The program is active and well-funded by most of the large accounting firms in Detroit and some local foundations. All of the major universities in the area now participate and most offer credit to student volunteers. The success of the Detroit program has come to the attention of foundation executives in other Michigan communities, with the likely result of additional organizations in the state.

The Hartford group started in 1970 under the active sponsorship of the Connecticut CPA Society. After languishing for lack of funds and community interest, the organization broke off its formal affiliation with the Society in 1974, became separately incorporated, and opened an office in the low-income area. Initial funding support came from the Connecticut Society, the AICPA and local accounting firms. Since then, the Connecticut group has concentrated almost exclusively on providing service to minority-owned small businesses.

The Charlotte organization started similarly under the auspices of the North Carolina CPA Society in 1969, and decided in 1975 to disaffiliate from that group. The primary emphasis is on taxpayer assistance, although some effort is devoted to nonprofit organizations and minority-owned small businesses.

Minnesota Accounting Aid Society, which received its first significant funding in 1975, has a balanced program helping taxpayers, nonprofit organizations, and minority businesspeople. None of the four existing organizations is significantly involved in the fourth element of the Des Moines program—financial counseling to low-income individuals.

Other Unfilled Needs

All of the programs described above involved substantial commitment and marked progress in the short history of organized pro bono efforts by the accounting profession. Each has had the noteworthy (but seldom noted) effect of forcing the profession's attention toward the difficulties of the disadvantaged among us, and has pointed the way for broadened efforts by others.

That there were other needs in the society for accounting services was plain in an educated reading of virtually any metropolitan newspaper on any day. One issue is exemplified by a long-simmering dispute in San Francisco over whether the construction of high-rise buildings in a downtown area would be beneficial or detrimental to residential-property taxpayers? Will the services required by this construction (transportation, police and fire protection, and so on) cost more or less than the additional property taxes it generates? Environmentalists and neighborhood groups were against the construction, and were bolstered by *The Ultimate Highrise,* a 1971 book by Bruce Brugmann and Greggar Sletteland. Their opponents, the major business groups, were heartened by a March 1975 report, made after a $250,000 study, by the San Francisco Planning and Urban Renewal Association (SPUR).[1] The two studies reached totally different conclusions, and left the citizens in confusion.

Behind the SPUR report were a five-member policy committee, a seven-member technical advisory subcommittee, and a twenty-six-member advisory committee. Participating consultants were from the fields of urban economics, transportation, municipal finance, architecture, and survey research. Even though their deliberations dealt with basic accounting concepts—costs and revenues—the only accountant among them was a licensed (not certified) public accountant, who was there by virtue of his membership on the city's Public Utilities Commission. Accountants could have been helpful (and still could be) by giving San Franciscans a basis for making a rational decision by providing the means of reconciling the methodology and assumptions of the two studies and some idea of the consequences of the alternatives.

Cost overruns, which generate loud public (and political) outcry and sometimes needless controversy, might prove more apparent than real if accurate assessment of costs and provision for contingencies were made in the first place. Whether it is the Alaska pipeline, the Pentagon's latest weapons system, or a domed stadium in New Orleans, the stories

1. See "Summary, Impact of Intensive High-rise Development in San Francisco" (San Francisco Planning and Urban Renewal Association, March 1975).

are much the same—and so are the causes: inflation, strikes, or delays due to shortages of materials or bad weather. Since none of these events is as rare as a tidal wave in Omaha, one might reasonably ask why they were not accounted for in the original projections. Unlike the first probe into outer space or a new type of aircraft or naval vessel, publicly funded construction projects are of this planet and are rarely unique. They should be susceptible to reasonably accurate cost estimations, but one study indicated that the margin of error ranges from 26 percent for highway projects to 114 percent for special projects; the average overrun for rapid transit projects was 51 percent.[2]

Would citizens who are called upon to accept or reject a specific project change their votes if they knew that it would cost 26 percent more than the original estimate? 51 percent more? 114 percent more? Since you can't fool all of the people all of the time, might not a project be defeated at the polls even if its costs were accurately projected, as the voters justifiably assumed that it too was substantially underestimated? Is this kind of cynical approach any way to run a country?

While much of cost estimation is the province of engineers, accountants could illuminate the financial factors. An intensive, comparative analysis of cost overruns on several public projects might reveal common areas of omission or underestimation, which might then be avoided in future proposals. If the accounting profession played a larger part in the assessment of those proposals, citizens might be able to cast their ballots with more confidence in the political process.

State taxation and spending is another rich but largely unexplored field for accountancy in aid of the general public's interest. In 1973, Governor Ronald Reagan sponsored a tax initiative, known as Proposition 1, in a state-wide special election in California. The measure sought to restrict state government spending by setting a limit on the amount of taxes that could be levied. It was opposed by many state legislators and the California Teachers Association and California State Employees Association.

The two sides in this controversy made wildly different claims about the potential impact of its passage. How long before the proposed spending levels would be reached? What were the potential effects on federal revenue sharing? On local taxing agencies? On various state aid programs? The antagonists could not even agree on the definition of "revenue" within the initiative—the key figure in calculating the limit on state spending in future years. Even the Governor himself publicly

2. L. Merewitz, "Cost Overruns in Public Works with Special Reference to Urban Rapid Transit Projects," BART Impact Studies, Working Paper No. 196/ BART 8 (University of California at Berkeley, November 1972.)

admitted he did not understand the language of the 5700-word proposition. Once again, although accounting concepts were clearly at the heart of the disputes, the profession was never called upon to analyze, explain, or reconcile the opposing claims so that the electorate could objectively compare them. Sensibly enough, the confused voters defeated the initiative.

Doctors, lawyers, and insurance companies—but so far, not accountants—are struggling with the crisis in medical malpractice insurance. As the number of claims, their average size, and insurance premiums have skyrocketed, doctors have responded with strikes, premature retirements, and an exodus to other countries. Although they are not yet obvious, the effects on the quality and quantity of U.S. medical care may well be devastating. The causes of this dilemma are complex, interrelated, and deeply rooted in the institutions involved. Doctors blame lawyers on the grounds that the contingency fee system encourages patients to sue (because they have nothing to lose) and sometimes results in huge legal fees. Attorneys defend the system as the only way to assure compensation for victims of malpractice who rarely could afford to pay a lawyer otherwise.

Struck by the rising frequency and size of claims, insurance companies have raised their rates astronomically—the immediate cause of the crisis. The question is, are those rates justified? This raises a whole series of questions that accountants can help answer: What are the average and range of claims for specific damages? What is the loss experience for each medical specialty? What percent of the settlements goes to the injured party and what percent to the attorney? What is the average rate and range of compensation for attorneys specializing in these cases? How do they compare with those in other fields of law? What would be the effect of reducing the period within which a claim must be filed? How will the proposed rates affect the availability of health services? How can a doctor start a practice if he must first pay $15,000 to $20,000 for malpractice insurance? What portion of the average doctor's billings, by specialty, represents malpractice insurance premiums?

The mediation of labor disputes could well be eased by the participation of accountants. Typically present in such disputes are crying needs for the mastery of technical financial issues and for recognized objectivity—needs that accountants are well-suited to fill, yet accountants are typically absent from the mediation or arbitration team.

Legislation and regulations that deal with financial considerations could profit from input from the profession recognized as expert in such matters. The costs, control, and impact of Medicare and Medicaid would have been far better understood had more accountants been involved in their drafting. More recently, the rash of local, state, and federal laws on campaign contributions and expenditure controls have resulted in massive confusion and conflicts which might have been avoided had the accounting profession been more actively involved in writing them. The practicality, enforceability, and consistency of the statutes presented problems that called for involvement of the profession—but the legislators did not call on it. Why?

The answer seemed to be that neither the formal nor the informal structures through which the profession had thus far offered its pro bono work lent themselves to meeting the new needs typified by these examples.

How, then, were they to be met?

___(3)___

API Organizes

Born of strange parentage—frustration and inspiration—API, the first public interest accounting organization of its type in the United States, opened its doors in April 1972 in San Francisco, California. The frustration arose because the founding group could at first find no channel through which to offer their training and experience in the search for solutions to pressing social, economic, and political problems. The inspiration came from Ralph Nader and a small army of legal service attorneys who, in the previous five or six years, had proven that changes could be brought about by dedicated people operating independently of their traditional professional structures.

Why Accountants?

Unlike medicine and the law, accountancy has no myth portraying its practitioners as crusaders charging forth to save society. The activities of the professional accountant offer no parallel to stirring courtroom appeals or life-saving emergency surgery. Although seemingly undramatic, accountancy involves integral components of most public policy issues: the investigation, analysis, and evaluation of data. More importantly, accountants are objective and independent—perhaps by inclination, perhaps by training, perhaps both. These qualities loom large in the historical development of the profession and are reflected in the code of ethics of the American Institute of Certified Public Accountants (AICPA). Without them, indeed, the accountant would have no significant role to play in our economic system.

Among the actors who might appear on the stage of public interest issues, the attorney is supposed to be an advocate; the economist, usually associated with a political or doctrinal position; engineers, work for industry. Entering on that stage, accountants can bring with them objectivity and independence, ingredients that are vital to the public's acceptance of what is presented to them but that, until now, have been largely unavailable. Accountants' representations are generally accepted as unbiased by the public, the government, and the sophisticated financial community alike. Since this is so despite the well-known financial stake that the accountant has in satisfying his fee-paying client, it should be all the more true where no financial incentives operate. Accountants today feel the need to join the legal profession in bringing their particular expertise to bear on policy issues as well as to change the stereotyped image of accountants as tight-lipped drudges in green eyeshades.

In the report of the annual Gallup polls of preferred occupations among students, accountancy is not even listed as a choice—either because it was not specified in the questionnaire or an insufficient number of those polled chose accountancy as a profession.

The Gallup Poll results were supported by another poll commissioned by the AICPA in 1972. The sample was drawn from people in the middle and upper income levels who indicated (by their reading habits) some interest in financial matters. Respondents were asked to give their opinions of CPAs in comparison with doctors, engineers, bankers, and lawyers. About half of the respondents rated accountants as maintaining high professional standards, roughly equal to the other professions except doctors, who were rated highly by 83 percent. Accountants were considered "careful and meticulous" by 68 percent, more than any of the other professions including doctors! Eighty percent would likely call on an accountant for assistance in preparing income tax returns as compared with 13 percent for lawyers. The respondents also appeared to be surprisingly well aware of the scope of services performed by CPAs and respectful of their competence in their work.

But there was more bad news than good. By the criterion of desiring to serve people rather than simply making the most money possible, accountants were ranked last. Accountants were also ranked last in making a vital contribution to society; last in being creative and imaginative; last in helping mankind or society; last in receiving nonmonetary rewards and satisfaction; and last in being public spirited. Accountancy did come in first in one thing—in being the last choice for a profession!

Both these polls pointed up a problem that is firmly linked to accountancy's image: the number and, especially, the quality of young people entering the profession. One factor that apparently inhibited able and committed students from choosing accounting as a career was its failure to fulfill their desires to participate in the decision-making processes of their communities and of society in general. Accounting had no way to compete with law and medicine in attracting the high-caliber student with a sense of social concern and responsibility. Furthermore, the profession offered no way for its retired practitioners to utilize—for their own satisfaction and society's betterment—the wealth of knowledge and experience they had accumulated.

As thoughtful accountants groped toward some mechanism for community service, image repair, and recruitment to assure the profession's future, they were not unmindful of the structural problems that beset the profession. Among these are potential government interference with accounting and auditing standards, quality control and peer review, formal recognition of specialists, auditors' responsibilities for investigation and disclosure of illegal corporate payments, and the increasing frequency of malpractice claims and awards. While the profession deals with these problems directly, their solution could also benefit from the indirect effects of participation in issue-oriented pro bono activities. Such work would broaden the public's perception of the spectrum of work that accountants are capable of performing. Even though accountability is the newest leitmotif of public officials and organizations such as Common Cause, incredibly, accountants themselves have been rarely called upon to help implement it. The demonstration of analytical skills in impartially considering public interest issues on behalf of previously unrepresented interests could result in the broader recognition of the comprehensive services that accountants offer.

Responding to these considerations, eleven professional accountants began meeting in San Francisco in October, 1971. The founding group of Accountants for the Public Interest (API) ranged in age from the early twenties to the early sixties. All but one were in public practice. Most were sole practitioners or partners in small accounting firms, but many had had extensive experience with national firms. Over the next six months, the group met frequently to develop plans, programs, and procedures. During that period the number of participants more than doubled as word of the group's efforts spread.

The first important issue faced was the scope of activities of the organization. The original premise was to provide accounting consulting services to other nonprofit organizations that were working on public interest issues, cases, or projects with accounting or financial elements, and that otherwise were unable to afford them. Such services would include investigation, analysis, and interpretation of the factors related to the issues under consideration.

Three other types of assistance were debated: helping disadvantaged owners of small businesses, preparing tax returns for the poor, and directly aiding nonprofit organizations with their internal accounting problems—systems installations, bookkeeper training, tax return preparation, and the like. A prototype of an organization doing these kinds of work in fact already existed, the Accounting Aid Society (AAS), which had been started in Des Moines earlier that year.

The San Francisco group, however, decided against a program patterned on AAS. Assistance to small business was already being provided by The Accountants Committee on Urban Action of the San Francisco

Chapter of the California Society of Certified Public Accountants, but over its three years had proven quite ineffective.

Tax assistance was vetoed because members of the founding group felt no enthusiasm for volunteering to work on evenings and weekends on the same matters that they dealt with during regular business hours.

Whether to assist nonprofit organizations in their internal affairs was a more complex question. The first consideration was the allocation of time and effort. While the nonprofit organizations plainly needed this kind of service, it could well overwhelm the capacity of API's staff and volunteers and thus prevent it from conducting its primary program. The second consideration was the lack of appeal for volunteers because, like tax assistance, this work was too close to that performed during regular hours to offer much satisfaction. Finally, there were alternative means of filling this need: its lack of controversiality meant that it could be undertaken by the organized profession through the California Society or its San Francisco chapter. Following its decision, the group strove, unsuccessfully, to persuade the officials of the organized profession in the state to undertake this program along with its assistance to small business. To inform potential board members, volunteers, and foundations about the new organization, a statement that summarized its goals and objectives was issued.

Organizing for Action

Once the founding group had settled on its program, it turned to organizing to achieve them. The members felt strongly that the technical nature of the work called for limiting the board of directors to practicing CPAs or educators in the accounting field. Not all APIs have followed this pattern. One group includes several representatives of the minority community and of potential client organizations on its board in an effort to balance the representation on the board.

An executive committee was appointed to exercise those functions that could not be done efficiently by the full board of directors. The committee, consisting of the four corporate officers and three at-large board members, undertook two major responsibilities. The first was the selection of clients and cases. The principal questions that arose in this connection concerned the ability to pay and the public interest nature of the matter. The second was the approval for the final written report on each case.

One of the most divisive subjects debated by the San Francisco group was whether to establish an honorary or advisory board of directors. Proponents hoped to attract influential accounting and business leaders who would add stature to the organization and enhance fund-raising efforts. Others feared that such a board would dilute the independence and influence of the organization. In their view even the threat of resignation of one of these members in connection with a sensitive or controversial case outweighed any advantage such a board could confer. After months of debate and behind-the-scenes maneuvering, the board remained evenly divided on this question. The proponents then withdrew the resolution in the belief that an advisory board could not function effectively with only a bare majority support.

It became increasingly clear during the first six months of discussion that no matter how large the group of interested participants, an organizer-leader was essential to reasonable progress. Although the decisions were to be group decisions, someone with time, energy, interest, and leadership ability had to take the initiative and accept responsibility for preparing a wide variety of detailed proposals. In addition, someone had to assume such "housekeeping" duties as setting meeting dates, finding meeting places, and preparing agendas. Limited funds and a light workload dictated hiring only a part-time executive director in the initial stages of API. While technical competence was not ignored, the search centered on administrative, communications, and fund-raising abilities, and on imagination and leadership. Until the scope and number of cases became too much for an executive committee to handle through a close review of workpapers and reports, the executive director's technical competence was less important than these other qualities. The executive director initially worked on a volunteer basis while he developed the funding for his own salary and the other expenses of the organization.

Although an organization of this type may function as an unincorporated association, formal incorporation offered many advantages. First, the laws of incorporation in California, as in many other states, are far more specific than are the laws for unincorporated associations. Banking resolutions, voting rights, responsibilities of members and directors, and other organizational matters can be settled by reference to existing statutes; an unincorporated association may have to spell out such matters in great detail in its governing instruments. Second, the corporate statutes specifically provide for limited liability of board members. Finally, because of the absence of limiting statutory language with respect to unincorporated associations, their applications for tax exemption probably receive more careful scrutiny by the Internal Revenue Service than do those of corporations.[1]

1. Most states require modest filing fees for incorporating. Conformed copies of both the articles of incorporation and bylaws must be filed with the exemption application to the Internal Revenue Service. Exemption applications should also be filed at the state level in those states that require them.

Another type of exemption may be necessary as well. The accounting profession is regulated in all states, and all professional accountants must be duly licensed to practice. The problem is that the state boards of accountancy were established to control the ethics and standards for profit-making activities; nonprofit accounting was never contemplated.

The application of some of the rules can be troublesome to a nonprofit group such as API. For example, in California, a licensed accounting corporation cannot advertise or promote its services and must use a name which contains the individual names of one or more licensed accountants. San Francisco API successfully sought an exemption from the state board based on the contention that it was not providing traditional accounting, auditing, and tax services. Subsequently, it was discovered that the board has no authority to regulate nonprofit corporations, although it is charged with overseeing all "accounting" services. While legislation may be required to resolve the conflict in California and other states, making state boards aware of programs and plans of APIs could help prevent, or at least simplify, problems in this connection.

With an organizational framework in place, API set out to recruit volunteers. The program contemplated that volunteers would perform most of the actual case work under the supervision of the professional staff and the overall control of its board of directors. Besides, volunteers would form a growing base of support for the program and the concept behind it. To convince the leaders of the profession and those who controlled funding sources of the merits of and need for the program, the organization had to attract the interest and commitment of significant numbers of professional accountants.

Any early doubts about the potential interest among other professional accountants were quickly put to rest. The problem, rather, was to utilize volunteers effectively in order to maintain their interest and commitment. Even so, explaining the concept proved much more difficult than anticipated. Because the profession was familiar with the types of work already being done by various accountancy groups, the explanations continually seemed to shift from what API did to what it did not do. During the organization's first five years, through contacts by board members and publicity generated by completed cases, approximately 200 professional accountants in the San Francisco Bay Area expressed willingness to participate in the program. Most of them worked in the field of public accountancy: some were individual practitioners and some were partners in small accounting firms; others were partners or staff members of medium-sized and national firms; and a small group came from private industry and governmental accounting.

In line with the avowed purpose of using the API concept to attract high-caliber students into accounting, the educational establishment in the San Francisco Bay Area was drawn into plans for the organization from the very beginning. Professors from several schools and colleges were asked to sit on the board of directors, and plans were undertaken to use student volunteers under the supervision of the staff and of professional volunteers. API explored the possibility that students could obtain school credit for work performed, and use their case work for the basis of the thesis for a master's degree.

Substantial difficulties in implementing these programs soon became apparent. The pressures of completing a case by a deadline frequently prevented participation by students whose time was limited. The level of sophistication or experience demanded by many cases also inhibited the use of students. Until the full-time staff was large enough to supervise student volunteers, such a program was severely limited. Nevertheless, the word about the organization quickly spread to many campuses in the Bay area, and invitations to speak began to pour in from accounting clubs and accounting scholastic organizations. An education committee was formed to further develop and coordinate API's activities within the educational community.

Support: Moral and Financial

The formal apparatus of the accounting profession includes the American Institute of Certified Public Accountants at the national level and the various CPA societies and their affiliated chapters at the state and local levels. Many of these organizations are significantly (and understandably) influenced by the large national CPA firms.

The founders of API realized that developing a working relationship with the governing bodies of the profession might be difficult. The very creation of API implied that the profession was not constituted to provide services in potentially controversial situations. In a profession whose hallmark is conservatism—at least as related to financial presentations—the leaders are traditionally conservative. And the youthfulness of the profession limited its recognition of its responsibilities to the public at large in this arena. "Steer clear of public controversy" might well have been one of the less controversial, generally accepted accounting principles. One-to-one service, in the legal aid mold, has until recently been the paramount expression of pro bono work by the profession.

In spite of these obstacles, San Francisco API pursued the recognition and support of the organized profession. The first step was to notify officials of the California Society of Certified Public Accountants about the existence of the group and its program. The support sought was of a general nature—recognition of the need for the program and encouragement of members of the profession in California to volunteer their time. The reception was less than enthusiastic, and a sort of *Catch-22* process set in. The board of the San Francisco chapter of the society told API to develop a "track record" and come back for reconsideration. After about a year and a half, an eminently good record was presented, again without success. The disappointment was all the greater because some form of support from the organized profession would clearly have been helpful in obtaining funds from foundations and support from the national CPA firms. The California society suggested that support first be sought from the national firms, and several of these firms suggested that they would be more inclined to offer support if the society first gave its approval!

Contacts made with the American Institute of Certified Public Accountants were considerably more productive. Two immediate achievements lent credibility to the organization and the movement: the AICPA consented to publish a story about San Francisco API in the national magazine of the profession, the *Journal of Accountancy,* and a senior vice-president of the institute agreed to speak to the first national conference on Public Interest Accounting, held in San Francisco in November, 1973. Moreover, two past presidents of AICPA serve on the board of the National Association of Accountants for the Public Interest (see p. 40); a commission was appointed to study the social responsibility role of AICPA; and the Institute has made its mailing lists and structures for communication and liaison available to the new movement.

Within sixty days of incorporation, the Stern Fund in New York City agreed to provide the entire $26,000 budget for the first year of operation of San Francisco API. While preliminary discussions with foundation executives indicated that continued funding was a strong likelihood, it also became clear that foundation support for the general operating budget of this kind of an organization would probably be limited to its first three years. Most foundations are not willing to fund any program indefinitely and insist that other forms of support be developed. Since the board of San Francisco API felt that long-term support must come from the profession itself, some 3,500 CPAs within a fifty-mile radius of San Francisco were solicited by mail. Less than 1 percent sent in contributions. An application was filed with the United Crusade but was turned down. Partial support was sought from the United States Department of Health, Education, and Welfare for funding of staff and expenses related to a series of cases in the health care field. This request was also rejected.

Solicitation of friends of board members of San Francisco API was modestly successful: in the first year about $7,000 was raised. Contacts were also made with all of the "Big Eight" national CPA firms in San Francisco, and meetings were held with their representatives. To lay the groundwork for appeals for funding and other support, the first series of meetings sought to inform the managing partners about the program, answer their questions, and deal with their concerns. API also explored the "loaned-executive" program, under which many large commercial and industrial enterprises provide staff for community projects and continue to pay their salaries for a limited period.

Open for Business

Now that overall direction, staff, and at least initial funds were in place, San Francisco API was ready to receive its first client. The scope of activities of the organization and its goals shaped the criteria for selecting its early clients. The same criteria apply today:

First, the client must be an organization involved in a charitable or educational endeavor.

Second, the client must be unable to pay for the services needed. Few prospective clients would have any difficulty in meeting this criteria because very few public interest organizations include the case costs (such as accounting consulting fees) of their projects in their budgets. This requirement was designed to prevent API from competing with a CPA firm for fee-paying business.

Third, the client must accept the fact that the work will be performed in an objective and independent manner.

Fourth, the client must agree not to edit or excerpt from the report without prior permission. This provision was intended to preclude misleading summaries or news releases that might not include the caveats, assumptions, or limitations contained in the original report.

Finally, the client must evidence a serious commitment to the project or issue involved.

Once a client organization qualifies for assistance, there remain questions about the case:

First of all, is it a public interest issue? That is, does it involve a matter of broad public concern rather than one in which only a small group stand to benefit?

Next, does API have the time and capacity to handle the case? Because most of the case work is performed by volunteers, thorough administrative consideration is required before acceptance of the case and thorough review for quality control is required after the report is finished, API cannot handle "emergency" cases. As a rule of thumb, API takes no case that has to be completed in less than sixty days. If a case should involve a highly technical matter in which specific industry experience is vital, it would be accepted only if such expertise was available from the volunteer or the paid staff.

In addition, does the client recognize the real needs for this specific case? Experience proved that the client often had only a general understanding of the issues involved and needed help in identifying and limiting the issues to be examined or data to be accumulated.

If a case met all these conditions, the arrangement with API was formalized by a letter of request for services outlining the specific assistance required and the terms under which it would be provided. One of the key provisions recognized API's right to release the report to the public should the client fail to do so because the findings were adverse to its position.

A final paragraph called for the client to submit an evaluation of the work upon completion of the case. Negative comments were helpful in correcting inadequacies. Praise of the work and the report were obviously helpful for publicity purposes and for appeals to potential sources of funding. During its first five years, San Francisco API received only one negative evaluation.

The preliminary case survey made before submission of the request to the executive committee included an estimate of the time and deadline requirements of the case. The executive director then assigned the responsibility for the project to one of the case supervisors and together they decided on the number of professional volunteers to be recruited for the case. This decision was based on the scope of the case, the total time requirements, the deadline, and the possibility of dividing it into segments. The supervisor then reviewed the volunteer files for those who were available and had the necessary background to handle the case.

By trial and error API learned to set realistic expectations for volunteers. The tax season presented problems for those in public accounting practice. But even then, and during the summer vacation months, such volunteers were still available. The built-in inefficiencies in utilizing volunteers also had to weigh in the decision to accept a case. The supervisor was encouraged to utilize student volunteers on those segments of the cases that were not highly technical and where their work could be closely supervised. Student assistance was most useful in research, fact gathering, and figure accumulations.

Virtually every case accepted by San Francisco API in its early years was unique. Indeed, this was what attracted the volunteers and maintained their enthusiasm. There were no previous workpapers to refer to, no cutting up of a draft of a report on a similar case to "write" a final report, and, for the most part, no textbooks on dealing with the specific case. On each case, therefore, the technical approach had to be newly decided.

Whenever possible, the team approach was used. The team generally consisted of the executive director, the supervisor, the volunteer-in-charge, and a member of the executive committee. The first step was a review of the letter of request, the engagement letter, and any other data submitted by the client. The next phase consisted of the accumulation of all available published and private data related to the subject. Along the way certain elements of the case were identified and could be worked on while the full scope of the work program was being determined. The basic consideration was always the final report. Flexibility to change tactics was preserved throughout this process. The unavailability of certain information might make it necessary to modify the direction of the work. In extreme cases, a proposed portion of the report might have to be omitted. On the other hand, sometimes the discovery of unexpected data resulted in the expansion of the scope and a change in direction of the final report.

If changes in work performed or the final report were significant enough, the client was notified. In a few cases the changes were so substantial that the assignment was terminated or a new agreement was written and approved. There were also instances in which the client's lack of interest or commitment to the study became so apparent that API considered the agreement broken and terminated the project.

Reports were given in writing whenever that was feasible. Besides avoiding misinterpretations and misunderstandings, and providing a permanent record, written reports permitted the application of quality control procedures. In certain cases, the nature of the assignment called for an oral presentation or report. For example, a consumer group requested assistance in rate hearings before the California Public Utilities Commission. In addition to written testimony, the case involved attendance at the hearings and ad hoc assistance to the client representatives in the examination of utility company witnesses.

Wherever possible the report was drafted by the volunteer in charge of the case. If the nature of the project permitted, each volunteer participant prepared his own section of the final report. The supervisor was responsible for the initial review, and the executive director conducted a final review of the workpapers and report before submission to the executive committee. The executive committee representative was kept current on all major developments during the field work and the report preparation. By this means the executive committee retained some contact with the work as it progressed and some input into the approach taken to both the field work and the report.

The executive committee's consideration of reports was extensive. Frequently, it sent the report back for major redrafting. The committee was concerned primarily with two elements: support for the information presented and the positions taken; and strict adherence to an objective, nonadvocative approach.

Nonadvocacy: Problem and Promise

The nonadvocacy of API was the subject of question by the media, doubt by some leaders of the accounting profession and deep concern by the organizers of San Francisco API. The board felt that the greatest contribution the organization could offer was their training, education, and experience in being objective. Indeed, API recognized the likelihood that its credibility could not survive taking advocacy positions. Therefore, other than in situations involving clear and obvious mistakes, the reports avoided categorical judgments on "right" and "wrong." Instead, they pointed out that there was more than one way to look at a set of figures and offered an alternative that was appropriate to the specific circumstances of the case at hand. Since protestations of objectivity never would satisfy the doubters, the reports had to be the final evidence of API's ability to maintain a nonadvocative position. Acutely aware of this situation, the executive committee was diligent in carrying out its review responsibilities.

Independence is the key to the credibility of public interest accounting organizations. Furthermore, it is the answer to those who accuse public interest organizations of "advocacy"—an accusation made with contempt or at least derision. Whether an API should defend itself against the charge, or proudly admit it, will be taken up in the last chapter. In any event, it is instructive to contrast the independence of an accountant in public practice with that of an API accountant. The independence and objectivity of the former are accepted with little question by the financial community and government agencies, an acceptance vital to the functioning of our economic system. A few skeptics question the ability of the accountant to render an adverse judgment in the performance of audits, because of his stake in a continuing relationship with the client, yet most people and most of the institutions of this country rely on auditors to perform objectively and independently even under those circumstances.

The issue has been sharpened, both inside and outside the profession, in connection with management advisory services. Many wonder how the members of an accounting firm can, in an audit role, objectively evaluate management when other members of the same firm have given advice and participated in management decisions of the client. Once again, the prevailing view is that they can.

The question of independence for an API centers around different considerations. First of all, neither the individual volunteer nor the organization has a financial stake in the work. Indeed, APIs do neither audits nor management advisory work. The questions here revolve around philosophy—and a bit of guilt by association. Anyone who assumes that those involved in an API hold the same social philosophies, political concerns, and economic theories need only attend a board meeting to be disabused of this notion. What the board members have in common is a pragmatic realism, concern for their communities and society, and a belief that those who cannot afford to pay for professional accounting services deserve some representation of their interests in the decision-making processes that affect them. They are not homogenous— racially, sexually, socially, or politically. Sometimes their collective decisions are contrary to the philosophy of some members of a board, or even of a majority.

Independence and objectivity are demonstrated first during the initial consideration of a request for help. Rigid adherence to the criteria for case selection eliminates nonobjective factors from the decision about taking the case. Independence also guides the rest of the performance, from the choice of procedures to the selection of items to examine or test. Objectivity becomes paramount in the written report on the case: words or phrases that express opinion or are not fully supportable are diligently avoided.

"Independence" and "objectivity" are used interchangeably here. "Nonadvocacy" might be a better word to apply to an API. The term was used in all of the early API literature, and it consistently raised more questions than it answered. Those who raised the question of the ability of API not to advocate while serving an advocacy organization were frequently those who stoutly defended their own objectivity in their audit activities. They failed to recognize that though API entered a case at the behest of a particular organization with its own point of view, API's purpose was not to support that point of view but to illuminate the issue for the public it affected. They also failed to give credence to the written engagement letter, which expressly acknowledges that the work will be done in an objective manner.

Would critics be stilled if the APIs operated without clients or agreements with other organizations, and instead initiated their own cases and studies? Some feel that the client and written agreement insulate APIs from charges of advocacy while others feel that guilt by association would be minimized if API had no clients. This, too, will be discussed in the last chapter.

Once again, the test must be performance. Only experience can prove that quality control and review procedures that constantly focus on objectivity, independence, and nonadvocacy can help an API avoid taking sides in an issue: that it can present facts and data, analyze and interpret information, offer alternative accounting treatments, and evaluate and reconcile conflicting presentations, without asserting, for example, that the airport cannot be expanded, or the utility rate should be raised, or the hospital should provide more free care to the indigent.

Facing Problems

Other problems—either real or imagined—became apparent as API organized and took on its first cases.

One problem held the threat of strangling the movement at its birth. Some accountants, out of unfamiliarity with the program or its goals, felt apprehensive that APIs would offer them competition, and for this reason withheld their support.

Paradoxically, the anxieties about competition are frequently expressed by stalwart defenders of the free enterprise system. Even if competition developed between the profit-making sector and the nonprofit sector in accountancy, it would not be unprecedented. It already exists in law, medicine, and research. For one example, the nonprofit Stanford Research Institute frequently competes with the profit-seeking Arthur D. Little Company. Competent antagonists rarely fear competition.

From the beginning, in any case, API has sought vigorously to avoid competition, as evidenced by its criteria for client eligibility and case selection. API was established to serve only those unable to pay for professional accounting services, to represent the previously unrepresented—in short, to supplement, not supplant, services available through commercial channels. The record supports the ability to fulfill these aims. In any event, the question has been purely theoretical since not so much as a whisper of a complaint has been raised about an actual act of competition.

An exception to this criterion was established by San Francisco API to accommodate those matters in which the client was unable to retain a CPA firm because of the controversiality of the issue. To date this provision has never been invoked. Either the client has been unable to afford professional services, or the controversial nature of the case has been no bar to his obtaining such services if he could afford them.

Far from competing, the work of an API has in several cases generated fees for a CPA firm. To cite one example, when the San Francisco Parent Teacher Association enlisted API in its attempt to understand the financial affairs of the San Francisco Unified School District, certain of the findings prompted the Board of Education to strengthen its management control system and resulted in a $50,000 fee to a national CPA firm.

In other cases, those who have opposed the position taken by an

API client have found it necessary to retain a CPA to help defend or develop their own positions. API activities might also highlight new areas of work for accountants, in which the need for their services and their competence have never before been recognized.

The question probably would never come up were the client-API relationship more like the traditional client-CPA relationship. In API cases, however, no fees change hands. The work (at least on issue cases) is not related to the client's own enterprise, and confidentiality is specifically disclaimed in the written contract. As in the case of objectivity, the best answer might be for APIs to find some means to participate in the consideration of public issues other than through clients.

Much discussion and confusion have surrounded another issue—the potential conflicts of interest that might confront an individual CPA or firm with some link to an API.

In an ethical sense, a conflict of interest exists when someone argues on both sides of a controversy or has a dual interest in a given transaction. The idea arises from the concept of faithful service to a client. It is a fiduciary principle, popularly expressed as "A man cannot serve two masters." APIs are unlikely to find themselves in such a situation. In connection with their activities, the simple terms "conflict," or "problem," or "client pressure" might be more accurate expressions.

Direct conflicts of interest are easily resolved. If a firm's client is involved in a controversy in which API is engaged by the opponent, API would avoid using any member of that firm as a volunteer on that case. Indirect conflicts of interest pose more complex problems. One would be solved if a member of the API board of directors abstained from the discussion and the decisions relating to a dispute involving his firm's client. Another falls under the heading of "client pressure": it arises when a firm gives financial support to an API that is opposing one of its clients in a specific controversy. If the client makes an issue of the matter, it can usually be resolved by reference to the purposes and procedures of the API. A firm that is accustomed to resisting such pressures in far more sensitive areas relating to audit reports and financial statements ought to be able to do so when it is merely the beneficiaries of the firm's charity that are questioned. The profession constantly attempts to confirm the belief of the business community, the Securities and Exchange Commission, and Congress in the profession's independence and invulnerability to pressure; the support firms give to an independent and responsible agency dedicated to representing the previously unrepresented can only reinforce those efforts.

Moreover, supporting an organization implies belief in its overall purpose and program, but not necessarily support for every action it takes. Many who support a political party (with time or money or both) take issue with some policy or program espoused by that party. Indeed, the opportunity to voice opposition to some aspects of that program may be the very reason for supporting the party in the first place. General approval of the goals of the American Civil Liberties Union may go hand in hand with strong disapproval of its filing a particular suit; and contributions to the United Way may be made despite distaste for the actions of some of its constituent agencies.

Today all major companies are extremely sensitive to their own public relations. Most managements are far more enlightened than they were ten or twenty years ago. It is extremely unlikely that management would seriously object to a firm's support of API—assuming that it knew about it, or that such objections would be a serious problem in any event, especially if most of the national CPA firms supported the same activity.

To put the matter in a different perspective, would a client be likely to complain if a firm gave 0.01 percent of its gross fees to a group that's trying to help the institutions in our society survive? Would it object if 0.1 percent of its employees volunteered 5 percent of their billable time— on their own time?

The legal profession once again offers an example in its handling of this question. Clearly, attorneys, who are by definition advocates, should have a more serious conflict of interest problem than does API, which has a policy and a record of not taking sides in an issue. Yet virtually every major law firm in the country supports one or more public interest law organizations. Board memberships of such groups as the Lawyers' Committee for Civil Rights Under Law, the Council for Public Interest Law, and others are heavy with the most distinguished legal names of the time.

A traditional ethic of the profession involves confidentiality of the client-accountant relationship. This is analogous to the attorney-client relationship, in all but one respect: it is not legally privileged from scrutiny.

Adhering to this conventional method of treating clients, API at first issued reports directly to clients, permitting them to control further distribution. At the first national conference (see p. 40), this policy came under severe criticism. How could API claim to represent a public interest if it allowed a client to suppress a report that attacked or failed to support its position? The only answer was to change the policy at the next API board meeting.

Doctors are not the only victims of skyrocketing malpractice claims and insurance premiums. CPAs have had much the same experience. The protection that disclaimed opinions or unaudited statements once afforded can no longer be depended upon, and the definition of negligence appears to be broadening.

Many prospective API board members and volunteers, therefore, were concerned about professional liability. The complexity of the answers matches the complexity of the question.

First, a distinction must be made between those engaged in public accounting practice and those engaged in industry, government, teaching, and so on. The former invariably have professional liability insurance coverage, while the latter rarely do. Even those who have insurance through their firms, however, may not be covered for outside activities.

As far as is known, no malpractice suit has ever been filed against a public interest organization, and public interest law organizations apparently view the likelihood of such a suit as quite remote, since few carry professional liability insurance. For one thing, few clients would wish to incur the unfavorable publicity that such a suit would attract. Furthermore, a jury probably would take into account that the work was done by volunteers and for a nonprofit organization, although those considerations would have no legal effect. In the special case of APIs, suits are all the more unlikely because APIs do not perform the types of work most often involved in accounting malpractice litigation—audits and tax consulting. In the end, however, the best means of forestalling malpractice suits is quality work, backed up by rigorous review procedures and carefully worded defensible reports.[2]

The National Breakthrough

San Francisco API was not content with helping to illuminate public policy issues, involving professional volunteers, and encouraging quality students to enter the accounting profession in the Bay Area alone. The founding group hoped to encourage others to start similar organizations around the country. The ultimate objective was to spur the accounting profession itself to deal effectively with large national issues. The first major step in this direction came as a direct result of the story about San Francisco API in the *Journal of Accountancy* of August 1973, which in turn generated stories about the organization in local daily newspapers, the *Los Angeles Times, Business Week, The Wall Street Journal,* and *Newsweek.*

These stories elicited scores of inquiries from major cities all over the United States, as well as a few from Canada and England. As a

2. Even an unsuccessful suit could be extremely damaging to an API. Therefore, the National Association of Accountants for the Public Interest (NAAPI) has arranged for insurance coverage for its affiliates, their board members, and volunteers. NAAPI itself is covered for $1,000,000. The relatively low cost of the insurance obviously reflects the underwriter's belief in the unlikelihood of a suit, and the satisfaction with API programs, controls, and performance.

result, it was decided to sponsor a National Conference on Public Interest Accounting which was held in San Francisco in November 1973. Sixty-five people from twelve states attended this two-day conference to hear more about what happened in San Francisco and how it had been accomplished. Many had been active in other kinds of public interest accounting organizations in their communities and wanted to share their experiences. Many who had previously worked with accounting aid societies, minority business assistance programs, or tax assistance programs left the conference determined to become involved in API-type organizations in their communities. During 1974, four similar organizations were started. From January of 1975 through January of 1977 ten additional groups joined in the growing movement.

The National Association of Accountants for the Public Interest (NAAPI) was incorporated in January 1975. Its members are individuals and accounting organizations that conduct volunteer assistance programs, and its board of directors consists of representatives from each of the existing API-type organizations, as well as interested individuals in other fields who may be helpful to the movement. NAAPI's primary goals are to support the programs of its affiliates, encourage the formation of new organizations around the country, coordinate cases of national significance, seek support from the organized accounting profession, and develop long-range sources of funding for the movement.

Thus NAAPI has become a prime vehicle through which accountants can express their social concerns and effectively participate in the solutions of the problems of our society.

____(Part Two)____

Getting Down to Cases

Introduction to Part Two

In today's complex society, public policy issues at every level of government usually contain financial or accounting elements. The case studies presented in chapters four through ten are intended to give some notion of the wide range of issue-oriented projects that lend themselves to accounting analysis. Obviously, the selection does not exhaust the possibilities.

The cases also illustrate the evolving approach, procedures, and controls of the still young public interest accounting movement. Although equally significant matters have been studied by the newer affiliates of the National Association of Accountants for the Public Interest, these cases were all handled by San Francisco Accountants for the Public Interest. They thus take advantage of the author's previous involvement with that organization and familiarity with the background of the cases.

_____(4)_____

The Hill-Burton Act

The New Orleans Case

In 1946, the first federal intervention to provide health care to other than the military forces was drawn up in the form of the Hospital Survey and Construction Act, which became known as the Hill-Burton Act. The legislation, which provided money for construction of hospital facilities, required institutions that received grants to serve all persons in their areas and to provide a reasonable amount of service to persons unable to pay. "Free patient care" was defined as hospital services offered below cost or free to "persons unable to pay therefor," including both the legally indigent and those who are otherwise self-supporting but are unable to pay the full cost of the care.

Later regulations issued by the Department of Health, Education, and Welfare set forth the level of service required in the "presumptive compliance guideline" as 3 percent of cost of operations (less that attributable to Medicare and Medicaid) or 10 percent of the grants received by the facility, whichever was less. Alternatively, a facility could certify that it would turn no one away. Then came the escape clause: a facility was allowed to provide even less service (presumably all the way down to zero) if it convinced the state agency, which held the authority to monitor the program, that it was not financially able to do more.

This question of "financial feasibility" lay at the heart of a case brought to San Francisco Accountants for the Public Interest less than three months after the organization opened its doors. The client organization was the National Health and Environmental Law Program, which subsequently changed its name to the National Health Law Program (NHELP).

Marilyn Rose was then a staff attorney for NHELP. From 1966 to 1968 she served as Acting Chief of the Health Branch Division of Civil Rights, Office of General Counsel of the U. S. Department of Health, Education, and Welfare in Washington. During this time a matter was brought to her attention concerning a hospital in North Carolina which

43

had received Hill-Burton funds and had made a commitment to provide free service to the poor as required by the Hill-Burton Act. The investigation of racial discrimination charges against the hospital indicated that it provided no free care and used economic justification for not serving blacks. She informed the Office of General Counsel of the Public Health Service within the Department of HEW that the civil rights investigation indicated that the hospital was violating its Hill-Burton commitments. No action was ever taken on this report, as later admitted by HEW.

Shortly thereafter she joined the staff of NHELP, first as Chief of Special Litigation and next as Washington Counsel. Her area of specialization was the development of the law to give the poor and indigent more access to health services. What she had learned about the North Carolina hospital during her work with HEW suggested that the Hill-Burton Act was a logical and fruitful means to that end. HEW had obviously never taken the Hill-Burton free service provisions seriously. Although the stated purpose of the legislation was to provide health facilities for the use of *all* people who might need them, for some twenty-five years it remained exclusively a program to support the construction of such facilities without regard to providing service to the indigent. The provision requiring a reasonable volume of service for persons unable to pay was apparently a means of dealing with political pressures. During the testimony before the Senate Health Subcommittee, Senator Robert Taft suggested the possibility of requiring that beneficiaries of Hill-Burton funds give a certain percentage of service to the poor. In an apparent compromise, the act permitted an escape from the free service requirement if the facility could prove that it was not "financially feasible." Since 1946, some 6,000 health institutions have received some 11,000 grants totaling over $4 billion and have given the specific assurance that they would provide a reasonable volume of free and below cost service to the poor.

A series of suits in the early 1970s revealed how the service aspect of the Hill-Burton program had been neglected. The first of these suits was *Cook, et al* vs *Ochsner, et al*, filed in July 1970 in the United States District Court in New Orleans, which charged that ten Hill-Burton hospitals in New Orleans were ignoring their commitments to the United States and the Louisiana state Hill-Burton agency with respect to serving the poor. The state agency was also named as a defendant and charged with failure to enforce the assurances, and in May 1971, HEW faced the same charge, as well as one of failing to develop standards for general enforcement. Marilyn Rose was chief counsel in this matter, which was brought as a class action by eight individual plaintiffs.

Rose early recognized the complexity and significance of a definition of "financial feasibility." She also recognized that this was an accounting matter with which she could not deal adequately, but her search for assistance in the Washington and New York areas proved unsuccessful. Finally, through a contact at the Urban Institute in Washington she heard about Accountants for the Public Interest in San Francisco. In several lengthy phone conversations in the spring of 1972, API learned that three of the ten hospital defendants in the case, Flint-Goodridge, Sara Mayo, and Methodist—claimed that they were financially unable to meet any commitment to provide free services to the poor. The ten hospitals all had received Hill-Burton funds, and all were either in New Orleans or neighboring Jefferson Parish, which NHELP considered the relevant geographic area. Flint-Goodridge was known as the black middle-class hospital; since token integration, it had apparently lost black patients without gaining any white patients. Sara Mayo, the only hospital that had served both races prior to the 1960s, had claimed that it served lower-income patients when it received a second Hill-Burton grant in 1968. Both hospitals had discontinued their outpatient service at the end of the sixties; Flint-Goodridge participated minimally in Medicaid, but Sara Mayo and Methodist, a new hospital in a new suburb, refused to participate at all.

In June 1972, Rose sent to SF API copies of the financial reports for the three hospitals, along with other materials. Rose closed her letter with the plea, "We need professional analysis of their accounts to determine the legitimacy of their financial feasibility arguments."

This case clearly met all of the criteria established by SF API. There was a nonprofit Section 501(c)(3) client; the case involved a public interest issue of great significance which would benefit from accounting analysis; and the client could not afford to pay for the services. Later in API's history, the early deadline—the case was to go to trial July 10—would have been a problem. At that stage, however, API had only a few active cases and volunteer time was available. The volunteer files held a considerable pool of interest, talent, and experience in the health care field. One of the volunteers was a former controller of a large hospital in San Francisco. Others were, or had been, associated with firms that had audited hospitals. Still others had extensive experience with Medicare cost reports for other types of clients in the health care field.

The Executive Committee accepted the case, agreeing in its formal letter to "review the financial reports of these hospitals to determine if they are financially able to provide free or below cost care . . . to consult with you by telephone . . . [and if necessary to send] one of our officers to New Orleans" for the trial.

Three volunteers worked on the case, each studying and analyzing the financial statements and records of one hospital. The co-executive directors took supervisory responsibility since they were the only paid staff at that time.[1] After the initial review by volunteers, the five-man team met several times to plan strategy and approach.

The data submitted included standard financial statements and Medicare cost reports for the three hospitals. The financial statements disclosed operating losses in most cases for most of the years under review. The pressure imposed by the impending court trial limited the detailed work that could be performed; however, the team had time to develop a few major points applicable to all three hospitals.

The first question was whether financial feasibility could be readily determined from the standard financial statements. This problem was complicated by the failure of the Hill-Burton regulations to define "financial feasibility."

The team believed that a cash flow statement might depict financial feasibility, within the implied legislative meaning of the term, more accurately than the accrual basis presented on the financial statements. Conversion of the data disclosed a positive cash flow for all of the hospitals for most of the years in question.

One of the major items involved in the conversion from an accrual to a cash basis was depreciation on buildings and facilities. Although depreciation was a legitimate expense for standard accrual-basis statements, the propriety of including it for purposes of determining financial feasibility was questioned. The data presented and the experience of the volunteers suggested that the hospitals were unlikely to fund their depreciation; that is, the replacement of facilities in all likelihood would be financed by private contributions or additional government grants. Under these circumstances, depreciation should not have been considered an expense in assessing financial feasibility. Furthermore, depreciation was taken on the assets acquired with Hill-Burton funds, in essence, to justify the inability to comply with the free or low cost care provision of the grant. This practice may be likened to having one's cake and eating it too.

Another major area of dispute involved the distinction between fixed and variable expenses. As in any enterprise, certain expenses of hospitals, such as administrative salaries, professional fees, insurance, and interest, are relatively fixed; an increase in activity will not raise such expenses significantly. Other expenses—food, supplies, and linen—are variable; they rise in proportion to an expansion in services rendered. Some expenses may fall between the two extremes and be considered

1. For the first several months of SF API's existence, two people served as co-executive directors.

semivariable, such as salaries of supervisors. A rough analysis of the hospitals' expenses indicated that a substantial part were fixed: they were incurred no matter how many—or how few—patients were served. For example, in one of the years in question in the case, Flint-Goodridge provided 37,895 patient-days of care at a total cost of $2,255,818, or an average of $60 per patient-day; its total variable expenses were $488,682, or an average of $13 per patient-day. Fixed costs per patient-day in this case were about three-and-one-half times variable costs. The significance of this calculation is that the hospital, operating at substantially less than optimal capacity (generally considered to be 85%), could have provided care to the poor at a charge of $13 per day, or could have taken half its poor patients for nothing and the other half at an average of $26 per day according to their ability to pay (or any variation that would average out to $13) at no additional cost to the hospital.

The accounting treatment of unrestricted contributions was also questionable. *The Hospital Audit Guide* required that such revenue be reported as income in the statement of revenue and expenses, since it is available for the same purposes as are patient revenues.[2] One of the hospitals in this case reported all of its contributions as restricted and therefore excluded them from the statement of revenues and expenses, thus eliminating them as a factor in the determination of net profit (read "financial feasibility"). From their experience, the volunteers knew that it was highly unlikely that all contributions would be restricted. SF API therefore suggested that the court require the hospitals to identify, substantiate, or verify their allocation of such contributions.

The final major point involved charity allowances, courtesy allowances, and bad debts. Charity allowances designate the billing value of free or below cost service; courtesy allowances are the billing value of allowances for reduced charges to employees, doctors' families, and the like; bad debts are business losses at billing value, suffered when customers—in this instance, patients—are unable to pay for contracted services. The failure to segregate these three distinct types of expenses not only made it difficult to evaluate the propriety of including such expenses for purposes of determining financial feasibility, but also made it impossible to determine the amount of services required under the law that had actually been provided—that is, the charity allowances.

The report to the court also stated:

The financial statements prepared by the hospitals, whether certified to by Certified Public Accountants or not, do not provide criteria for the determination of the financial feasibility of providing free or below cost service within

2. American Institute of Certified Public Accountants, Committee on Health Care Institutions, *The Hospital Audit Guide, 1971–72.*

the meaning of Hill-Burton obligations.   This is not intended as a criticism of
the financial statements.[3]

The assistance resulted in all the hospitals agreeing to provide a certain
amount of free care.   In August 1972, the court-approved consent agreement directed the hospitals to supply an aggregate of $983,000 of free or
below cost service to the indigent during a twelve-month period following
the order.

The New York Case

A few months after the conclusion of the New Orleans case, San Francisco API received a request from MFY Legal Services Inc. of New York
city to study the financial data of Beth Israel Hospital in New York with
respect to their compliance with the Hill-Burton Act.   This case was
also accepted.

A brief report to the client listed some intriguing points uncovered
in the investigation:

We have examined the financial information submitted by Beth Israel Hospital and have the following comments:

1) If the outpatient department of the hospital was discontinued during
   1971, how is it that the costs during the first half of 1972 were more than
   half the cost during the year 1971?
2) Bad debts as reported by the hospital seem very high.   You will probably need a breakdown of such reported costs for 1971.
3) If the outpatient department is being cut back, why should the cost
   allocation for 1972 be the same as for 1971?
4) You will probably need a statement for 1972 to date, so that current
   costs can be analyzed.
5) Because of the complexity of the operation and the financial statements, it is clear to us that the accounting analysis cannot be handled
   on a long-distance basis.   If you proceed, you should get local
   assistance.

In conclusion we would like to point out that if your suit is based on the
Hill-Burton Act and compliance therewith, there may be one basic problem.
In the New Orleans case, you may know, the hospitals were directed to render
free or below cost service to the indigent to the extent of from 5 percent to 10
percent per annum of the Hill-Burton grant.   In the case of Beth Israel Hospital, this would amount to a top figure of $40,000 per annum (10 percent of
the full grant, $400,000, not all of which has been received by the hospital).

3. "Report on Financial Feasibility of Providing Free and Reduced Cost Care"
(API, July 11, 1972).

Although we do not presume to offer a legal opinion on this matter, it is our firm conviction that from an accounting point of view, it would be impossible in an operation of the size and complexity of Beth Israel to prove that the hospital is not rendering free service of less than $40,000 per annum. We do not mean to discourage your efforts, but we do feel we should express our opinion on the accounting realities. If we can be of any further help, please do not hesitate to write again.

San Francisco API thus gave a clear illustration of its objectivity and independence. The analysis indicated that the client did not have a good case from an accounting standpoint. The client won certain legal issues not related to the accounting problems, but did not proceed on claims relating to accounting matters.

Later Developments

API's involvement with the Hill-Burton cases did not end with the New Orleans and New York matters. In April 1974, Marilyn Rose, now affiliated with the Center for Law and Social Policy in Washington, asked for assistance in contempt proceedings brought against several of the New Orleans hospitals which signed the consent decree, for failure to comply with the court order to provide a specified amount of free care. The question of financial feasibility arose again with respect to one of the hospitals which had not earlier raised financial inability as a defense.

API found that some of its original comments on this question were applicable to the current situation. One new point was the inclusion in the financial statements of approximately $85,000 for the loss on sale of miscellaneous equipment. API questioned the inclusion of this expense for financial feasibility purposes since it did not represent an expenditure of the current year.

The major issue, however, was the method chosen by the hospital, for measuring the dollar amount of free care provided. The hospital had claimed as one of the items representing free care, the difference between the operating costs of an outpatient clinic and the revenue received from it (comprising the nominal fees received from poor patients).

While API's report recognized that this generally was a legitimate approach, some other questions were raised:

Under normal circumstances, the measure of free or below cost care of a clinic facility would be the difference between the operating costs of the facility and the revenue received therefrom. However, in the instant situation, there appears to be a serious underutilization of the clinic as witnessed by the following acknowledged data:

Cost—outpatient clinic	$43,166.00
Occasions of service	599
Average cost per unit	72.06
Occasions of service	599
Divided by number of days	365
Number of patients per day	1.64

The above information reflects either serious underutilization of the clinic or possible overallocation of the costs. It would appear that rather than consider the net cost of the clinic as a measure of free or below-cost service, it would be more appropriate to consider the full charge for services rendered in the clinic less actual revenue collected for the year ended July 30, 1973. That figure is $4,683 (billing of $6,740, less revenue received of $2,057).

At the hearing, API's representative pointed out an anomaly in the hospital's system of measuring this item of free or below cost service. Since the costs of the outpatient clinic were fixed, an increase in utilization by patients (and, therefore, a corresponding increase in *real* care provided) would result in a larger offset to the clinic costs and, therefore, a lower amount of "free care" claimed! Conversely, a reduction in the number of patients served would result in a corresponding increase in the claim for free service. The ultimate illogic of this method was described by assuming that no patients were treated at the clinic—the result would be the maximization of the free service claimed up to the total amount of the cost of the clinic.

A representative of SF API helped the attorney in the examination and cross-examination of witnesses at the hearing. The report and testimony also resulted in the court rejecting claims of old "bad debts" for services rendered before the consent period.

In early 1975, the federal judge held certain hospitals in contempt and dismissed the cases against other hospitals.

An interesting by-product of these cases and their possible ramifications was evidenced by a case brought to San Francisco API by the Alameda County Legal Aid Society. A hospital in the county sued an indigent woman for failure to pay a $2,000 bill; both the hospital and the patient had expected that her bill would be covered by California's Medi-Cal program (part of national Medicaid). Since the hospital was the recipient of Hill-Burton funds, the attorney in charge of the case decided to investigate the applicability of the free service provisions of the act. Through a request for fiscal information, the hospital learned about API's willingness to assist counsel in evaluating the financial data of the hospital and its compliance with Hill-Burton. The hospital's concern about its compliance with Hill-Burton was apparent from its immediate withdrawal of the action against the woman.

The most recent of San Francisco API's Hill-Burton activities was the testimony given at public hearings in early 1975 on the proposed regulations of the California Department of Health, the state Hill-Burton agency. At the conclusion of the hearings, API was asked to submit a report concerning the regulations along with recommendations for revisions.

In the report, API pointed out that one of the regulations would have the effect of allowing health care institutions to choose between providing care to the qualified indigent and lowering charges to patients who can afford to pay for care (and who have already benefited from the availability of the facilities financed by Hill-Burton). Moreover, the proposed regulations ignored the factors (discussed in connection with the New Orleans cases) to be taken into account in assessing financial feasibility.

API also called for the exact opposite of one of the proposed regulations, which would have forbidden the state's department of health from re-examining any contract entered into by a hospital with another health care facility with a view to evaluating the hospital's ability to provide free or low cost care. It took serious issue with a regulation that expressly denied the appropriateness of the department's concern with the financial management of individual facilities. Taken together, the report noted, these four provisions constituted "a blank check to facilities [to] make whatever wasteful, lavish, imprudent or collusive arrangement [they wish]." ("Wasteful," "lavish," and "imprudent" were words that had been used in the proposed regulation to describe precisely those operations that the department could *not* investigate!)

API also called on the department to go beyond financial statements in determining financial feasibility, and to consider as well the depreciation of buildings, especially in connection with the source of funds and the method of depreciation; to exclude other noncash deductions; to distinguish charity allowances; to segregate restricted from unrestricted contributions; and to evaluate fixed versus variable expenses.

The necessity for involvement of API-type organizations in Hill-Burton matters may be seen from a report by the General Accounting Office (GAO), which reviewed various aspects of the Hill-Burton program during the summer of 1974, at the request of the Subcommittee on Health of the Senate Committee on Labor and Public Welfare. GAO investigators visited nine state agencies to determine how the free service requirement was being implemented. With respect to the agencies' evaluation of hospital performance, they found:

The evaluation function is essentially accomplished by matching the amount of free services required with the amount of free services provided as shown on financial statements submitted by the facility. None of the state agencies reviewed had an active program for verifying the information submitted by the facilities. Officials at three state agencies told us that they do not have sufficient personnel to conduct site visits to determine the facility compliance. Most of the state agencies reviewed planned to rely on complaints as an indication of noncompliance.

Barring a complete change of HEW policy, such complaints are likely to be pursued only by the public interest law firms concerned with health matters. The expanded involvement of public interest accounting organizations will be an important element in the success of attempts to utilize the existing legislation to effect significant improvements in the access of the poor to health care in the United States.

_____(5)_____

Care for Dependent and Neglected Children

Each year about 1,400 dependent and neglected San Francisco children enter Youth Guidance Center solely for emergency shelter care.[1] These are children who have been abandoned or abused; whose only parent is injured or has suddenly taken ill; or who themselves are considered dangerous. They become dependents of the Juvenile Court and remain at the Center for periods ranging from one day to several months, depending on how long it takes to make a decision about long-term placement.

The same facility is used for the care and detention of delinquent wards of the court. Under California law, however, dependents are separated from delinquents in housing, eating, schooling, recreation, and other activities.

The system of handling dependent children gives little consideration to the trauma that inevitably accompanies separation from the family environment. Even if it seems that the dependency will be temporary, no attempt is made to keep the family together by, say, providing a homemaker to take over for a sick parent, or placing siblings in one foster home. Responsible authorities also do not try to locate a friend or neighbor to care for the child so that he can attend the same school and thus minimize his adjustments.

Section 600 of the Welfare and Institutions Code of the State of California states:

Any person under the age of 18 years who comes within any of the following descriptions is within the jurisdiction of the juvenile court which may adjudge such person to be a dependent child of the court.
a) Who is in need of proper and effective parental care or control and has no parent or guardian, or has no parent or guardian willing to exercise or capable of exercising such care or control, or has no parent or guardian actually exercising such care or control.

1. San Francisco Juvenile Court Annual Report, 1969: 1,611; 1970: 1,288; 1971: 1,435.

b) Who is destitute, or who is not provided with the necessities of life, or who is not provided with a home or suitable place of abode.
c) Who is physically dangerous to the public because of a mental or physical deficiency, disorder, or abnormality.
d) Whose home is an unfit place for him by reason of neglect, cruelty, depravity, or physical abuse of either of his parents, or of his guardian or other person in whose custody or care he is.

A New Opportunity

In 1972, the San Francisco Foundation received a bequest of $225,000 to plan and provide new services for dependent and neglected children in the city. The foundation subsequently invited representatives from about twenty-five local agencies that serve children to discuss plans for implementing the bequest. This seemed a golden opportunity to mobilize the community behind an effort to improve the archaic and callous method of serving these children.

In January 1973, the Youth Law Center asked San Francisco Accountants for the Public Interest to prepare a cost comparison between foster care and homemaker services. Once the foundation group began to meet that spring, YLC asked API to modify its approach to determining the sources and uses of all the monies annually spent in the city for the care, treatment, and protection of neglected and dependent children.

The peculiar value of API was strikingly demonstrated in the concluding paragraph of the letter:

We propose that our offices work together on this analysis, it being our responsibility to determine whether federal, state and local laws, ordinances and regulations will permit the diversion of money from existing funding sources to support the new project, and it being your responsibility to identify the nature and amount of those sources and the purposes for which the monies are now being spent.

The Case

Since these new aspects of the case were merely a modification of the previously approved study, the API executive committee required no new engagement letter.

As two volunteers and a staff person met with the client and the members of the foundation's planning group, several things became clear. First, the initial report would have to be limited to the costs of maintaining the existing system. Time constraints made it impractical to determine funding sources—and such information would have been only peripherally important at that time. It was also clearly impractical to estimate the costs of alternative programs to use existing funding until the client settled on a specific plan. Second, the financial reports and records of the city of San Francisco would provide no quick answer. The city used a line-item budget and had no "cost center"—an accounting device to accumulate the costs for a program or department—for the care of dependent children. Furthermore, ten private agencies and city departments were sharing the costs of the existing system. Police officers picked the children up at their homes and delivered them to Youth Guidance Center; they were examined at a public hospital and given medical and dental care there; public school teachers taught them; utilities were supplied through the Public Utilities Commission, and so on. To identify all of the cost components, API relied on conferences and telephone calls with those knowledgeable about the procedures used and the agencies involved. Each of the ten was considered a cost center. Responsibility for identifying and allocating expenses for each was divided among the three assigned accountants.

Because the largest share of the costs of caring for these children fell on the city, API's approach was to compile data for the city's latest fiscal year, which had ended on June 30, 1972. Two of the private agencies involved had different fiscal years; because their costs were less than 10 percent of the total for all agencies and departments and because their programs were relatively constant during the periods in question, their "different-year" costs were included in the report, accompanied by a qualifying footnote.

One of the biggest expenses was salaries in Juvenile Hall (the center's reception and temporary detention facility) and in the Probation Department. Although the specific positions relating to dependent care were easily identified, the salaries paid for them were not readily available. They were estimated by applying the percentage of total actual salaries to total budgeted salaries for the respective divisions to the budgeted figures for those specific positions.

The report that San Francisco API made (reproduced below) was intended as a rough approximation of the total costs for care of dependent and neglected children in San Francisco in an effort to guide the planning of an alternative program. The assumptions and methodology used for each cost element were carefully spelled out. The figure was put at $2.85 million; but the initial estimates could be refined as more demographic data were developed and existing programs were more carefully defined.

In retrospect, API felt that additional time might have been sought for analyses of the number of dependent children dealt with through examination of police department records, foster care placement documents, and other data, to arrive at more reliable estimates. Barring that, the report might have indicated a range of costs between the likely minimum and maximum instead of pinpointing one number.

The Report

In accordance with your request, we have developed estimated costs for the emergency care of dependent, abused and neglected children in the City and County of San Francisco for the year ended June 30, 1972. A summary of our findings is presented in Exhibit A attached.

A brief description of the bases for the estimated figures follows:

Youth Guidance Center

Two programs are administered here, care of delinquents and care of dependents. The center maintains ten cottages, of which two are devoted to the care of dependents, and eight to the care of delinquents. Consultations with the Assistant Chief Probation Officer resulted in a decision to allocate expenses between the two programs in several different ways:

1. Certain expenses were connected in their entirety with one or the other program and were treated accordingly.
2. Some of the permanent salaries were directly attributable to the dependent program and were included in our summary together with a proportionate share of related expenses such as overtime, temporary salaries, etc.
3. Some expenses, such as foodstuffs, material and supplies, etc., were allocated to the dependent care program at 20% of total, on the theory that 2 of the ten cottages were devoted to dependent care.
4. Where none of the above criteria seemed appropriate, allocations were made on the basis of the judgment of the Assistant Chief Probation Officer.

We are not submitting with this report a detailed listing of these allocations, but our workpapers are available for your inspection.

Foster Grandparents Program

This program attempts to improve the child's life adjustment by having senior citizens visit them in the institutions where they are housed. It is funded by grant from the Department of Health, Education and Welfare of the Federal Government, administered by the San Francisco Family Service Agency. The cost of this operation was obtained from the administrator of the program and is related solely to the dependent care program.

Educational Costs

The San Francisco Unified School District figures were based on information provided by the District's fiscal office for educational costs of the Youth Guidance Center and were allocated to the dependent care component based on the 20% factor previously discussed.

Mt. St. Joseph's Home

The costs related to dependent care at Mt. St. Joseph's Home were developed from internal statistics maintained at the Home and its annual audit report.

Utilities

These costs were supplied by the San Francisco Public Utilities Commission. We have assumed that 20% of the total cost, $46,000, is applicable to the dependent care program.

San Francisco Department of Social Services

This department, in the case of voluntary referrals, attempts to resolve the problem without foster placement. Where such resolution is not feasible, the Department finds suitable placement in foster homes or institutions. Once placement has been made, the Department maintains contact with the children, the parents and the institutions.

The costs were supplied by the Family and Children's Division of the Department of Social Services. On the basis of information supplied by D. S. S., it appears that, of the seventy employees involved in the operation, twelve are concerned with temporary placement. Consequently, we have considered that 12/70 of the total cost of $1,059,590, or $181,644, is applicable to temporary dependent care.

Health Services Provided by the Department of Public Health

These services consist of medical, dental and psychiatric treatment at the Youth Guidance Center, San Francisco General Hospital and other institutions. Data was obtained from the Department of Public Health and expenditure reports of the City and County of San Francisco. We have considered that 20% of the total costs are applicable to the dependent care program, except in the case of psychiatric services, of which 5% are deemed so allocable.

Temporary Foster Care

These costs were estimated by examination of total foster care costs (temporary and long-term) contained in the records of the City and County and allocation of 10% of those costs to the temporary care component based on consultation with city personnel knowledgable in this field. No analysis of the foster care population is currently made and the distinction between temporary and long-term care appears to be quite subjective.

Police Department

These costs relate to answering calls and picking up and delivering children to San Francisco General Hospital or Youth Guidance Center. An official in the Police Department estimated that 1% of their total expenditures of $47,425,000 was allocable to the "Section 600" children here being considered.

Rental Factor

A factor of 50 cents per square foot per month was estimated by an architect to be a fair rental value of the Youth Guidance Center facilities. The buildings involved contain an estimated 50,000 square feet of space, of which an estimated 20% is deemed allocable to dependent children.

❊   ❊   ❊   ❊

Because of the involvement of Federal, State and City agencies, as well as private sectors of the community, it is possible that some expenditures may have been omitted.

Lacking clarity as to how you wish to relate various costs to categories of population served, we have not attempted to develop a per capita cost figure. We have some statistics and expect more. Once you have made your needs clear to us, we should be able to provide the needed information.

Because of time limitations, we have not analyzed the funding sources; i.e., how much money comes from where. This can be the subject of a separate study if you so desire.

It should be noted that, even if alternative methods of caring for dependent children are adopted, some of the expenses detailed in Exhibit A (p. 59) would continue. This should be carefully considered in projecting estimated costs of alternative programs. When in the future you determine what alternative plan or plans you intend to explore, please feel free to call upon us for help in estimating costs of such plan or plans.

The figures presented in Exhibit A were taken from the sources indicated above, and no auditing procedures were applied to them, so that no opinion is expressed by us as to the fairness of the figures.

The Client's Evaluation

San Francisco API received the following letter from the Youth Law Center after the issuance of the report.

We are happy to provide you with an evaluation of the above study, which was carried out at our request for the benefit of the San Francisco Foundation's Coleman Project.

The assignment was to determine the amount of money being spent by the city and county of San Francisco for the care of dependent and neglected children during the crisis period between the time that the children are placed in temporary detention and the time when they are either returned home or placed in foster care or other longer term arrangements.

As usual, it was impossible to determine this cost on the basis of any official budgets of city departments, because these costs are not isolated in those budgets.

Your accountants discovered that the program was being paid for by five different city departments, and a number of private agencies. It was necessary for your accountants to study each of those agencies, interview their administrators, and make informed allocations of all sorts of costs.

EXHIBIT A

Estimated Cost for the Care
of Dependent, Abused and Neglected Children
Year Ended June 30, 1972

Youth Guidance Center:		
Juvenile Hall Expenses:		
Salaries and Related Expenses	$305,000	
Other Expenses	31,000	$ 336,000
Probation Office Expenses:		
Salaries and Related Expenses	372,000	
Maintenance of Minors in Foster Homes	314,000	
Other Expenses	17,000	703,000
Total Youth Guidance Center Costs		$1,039,000
Foster Grandparents Program (Note 1)		146,000
Educational Costs		71,000
Mt. St. Joseph's Home (Note 2)		133,000
Utilities		9,000
Department of Social Services		182,000
Department of Public Health		54,000
Temporary Foster Care		685,000
Police		474,000
Rental Factor		60,000
TOTAL		$2,853,000

Note 1—Represents costs for the fiscal year ended February 28, 1973.
Note 2—Represents costs for the calendar year 1972.

All of this was accomplished in a remarkably short time, and produced a report containing facts which otherwise would have been available only to the public agencies themselves.

Since the Coleman Project hopes to use these same public monies in the future for its own operation, the report was truly invaluable to the planning process. Ordinarily, it is only the public agencies themselves who are able to develop this kind of information, because of the inherent limitations in the types of budgets which they publish. Thus, this is a fine example of how Accountants for the Public Interest makes it possible for citizens groups and community agencies to negotiate with government on a more equal basis.
Thank you very much for your help.

Conclusion

A nonprofit organization, Coleman Children and Youth Services, was formed in early 1975 to use the bequest to plan a comprehensive emergency system of housing and services in order to minimize the institutionalization of dependent, neglected, and abused children at the time of crisis. Its initial report, designed to indicate the characteristics of the children and of the admitting patterns, was based on a detailed and computer-tabulated analysis of all admission sheets within a fifteen-month period. Some of its findings were startling.

- Nearly half of the children were five years of age or under, and 36 percent of the children were white; they came from all over the city.
- About two-fifths were admitted because of "absent parents";
- One quarter required immediate medical attention;
- Admissions on weekends were half those on weekdays;
- 42 percent were released within three days.

Armed with these data and the San Francisco API cost estimates for the existing program, the organization was in a position to mount an effective campaign to convince the political leaders, city officials, and concerned citizens that more humane treatment of these unfortunate children was feasible. The results of these efforts were still not certain at the end of 1976. Hearings had been held at City Hall and citizen efforts were being mobilized. A start has been made, however, and a concerted attack on the problem has been assured.

___(6)___

Political Campaign Controls

Corruption has come a long way since the apple. Today's complex society offers endless breeding places for the infection and mass communications have propagated it.

The tax laws alone have fostered a national epidemic whose severity ranges from fudging on expense accounts to massive evasion. Improvements in communication have made it possible both to deceive more effectively and to publicize that deceit, thereby reducing confidence in our institutions. Polls in recent years reveal a woeful lack of trust in politicians, business, and the press.

Political corruption seems to lie at the heart of the matter. It takes votes to get elected, and it takes money to get votes. The attractions and expense of television advertising have spawned tremendous increases in the costs of campaigns and large contributions have become correspondingly vital. Understandably, many contributors of large sums expect a quid pro quo from the winners they have backed. Donors have learned, moreover, to cover all bases by helping more than one serious candidate—even in primary elections.

Not all donors look on their contributions as an outright purchase of support vital for their interests. Many expect nothing at all. Probably the most prevalent hope is merely to ensure the opportunity to be heard—quickly and seriously. This subtle advantage may be the most insidious of all. Listening to a constituent's problems is not dishonest or even dishonorable. The danger lies in "preferential listening" which is largely undetectable and which is denied to all but a few of the constituency. Even the unspoken threat to withhold financial support must weigh heavily in the office holder's decisions.

Business corruption runs the gamut from fraudulent advertising to industrial espionage to illegal campaign contributions. Here it is the relationship between business and government that seems to concern the public most. The issue may be a route decision by the Civil Aeronautics Board, a license from the Federal Communications Commission, the choice of weapons systems, investment credit for the utilities industry, oil import quotas, air-quality standards for automobile emissions—the examples are infinite. But the common denominator is influence, and the means through which it is exercised is money—campaign contributions, legal or illegal, direct or indirect.[1]

The San Francisco Effort

Even before Watergate, local and national efforts were under way to come to grips with the problem of campaign contributions and expenditures. San Francisco was one of the first major cities to pass legislation in this field, under the impetus of considerable pressure from a citizens group called the Coalition of San Francisco Neighborhoods (CSFN). The coalition is a natural outgrowth of the city's unique geographic and ethnic character. San Francisco is composed of distinct neighborhoods which are defined geographically and sometimes ethnically. Virtually all have formal or informal associations to lobby in behalf of their special interests. Some have existed for a century. During 1970, a citizens' initiative on the ballot sought to limit high-rise construction in San Francisco. Although the proposition lost in a close vote, the effort spurred city officials to take action on a city-wide urban design plan establishing zoning restrictions. The debate on this master plan quickly developed into disputes between neighborhoods since some felt they were being treated less fairly than others. As it became apparent that fragmented opposition to local government policies would be hopelessly ineffective, the CSFN was formed to mobilize concerted pressure from all of the neighborhoods on city officials.

The first effort of the coalition was directed toward changing the city charter to provide for district elections for members of the Board of Supervisors (the equivalent of a city council). Up until that time, candidates had run at large, and the high cost of running for city-wide office seemed to limit the choice of the electorate to the wealthy, and to plant seeds for favoritism, influence peddling, or worse. From the middle to the end of the sixties, the cost of an average successful campaign for the board had quintupled—from about $20,000 to about $100,000. Who was financing political campaigns, how much was being spent, how was it being spent and how was it being reported? No local ordinance demanded answers to these questions. The only controls imposed on local candidates were the laws of the state—which can be charitably described as confusing and inadequate. In mid-1973, under intense citizen pressure, the Board of Supervisors passed a campaign control ordinance requiring all local candidates and proposition campaigns to file statements of campaign income and expenditures. The aim was to

---

1. The author knows of one large corporation in which management "unofficially" informed all employees earning over a certain amount that they were expected to donate a specific percentage of their salary to a fund for support of selected candidates and issues.

place realistic and enforceable limits on the amount individuals may contribute to and expend in political campaigns in municipal elections, and to require full public disclosure of campaign contributions received, the names and addresses of contributors to such campaigns, and the purpose and amounts of expenditures.

However, a provision that would have required each campaign to use a trust account at its bank to establish an impartial review of the handling of campaign funds, and to make sure that the law was followed, was eliminated from the final legislation. There was thus no way to judge whether a campaign was handling its funds within the intent of the law.

CSFN set out to fill the breach. First they unsuccessfully sought volunteers from the San Francisco Chapter of the California Society of Certified Public Accountants to audit the books of campaigns requesting such help. Next, they turned to API to devise "a model set of standards and forms for campaigns so that books that are auditable may be easily set up."

The case met API criteria. CSFN was a nonprofit organization attempting to illuminate a nonpartisan issue that had wide public impact and to which accountancy could make a valuable—indeed, indispensable—contribution. The executive committee accepted the case immediately and assigned three volunteers. They defined their objective as providing a model format that would give interested citizens and groups a basis for comparing campaigns and that would facilitate independent audit verification of campaign statements.

The basic mechanism of the law was the filing of campaign statements—itemized reports of the required information—verified by the candidate and his campaign treasurer. Reports were to be filed between the twenty-second and eighteenth day preceding the election; between the seventh and fifth day preceding the election; within thirty days after the election; and every six months following the election if contributions were received or expenditures made during that time or if the unexpended balance of contributions exceeded $100.

The statements were to contain the cumulative total of all contributions and expenditures; "the full name, complete mailing address, occupation, principal place of business and name of employer, if any, of every contributor, the amount and form of every contribution" for every contributor of $50 or more (cumulative). They were also to report the "name and address of every recipient (of disbursements), the date and method of payment and the purpose of each expenditure."

A contribution meant a gift, subscription, loan advance, deposit, pledge, contract, agreement, or the granting of discounts or rebates not available to the general public. In the determination of the maximum permissible amount of contributions, gross revenues from fund-raising events could be reduced by direct, out-of-pocket costs, but not by more than 10 percent.[2]

With the exception of the candidate and his immediate family, no individual donor was permitted to contribute more than $500. A maximum of $2,500 was set for total contributions by the candidate and his immediate family. The maximum aggregate contribution was computed by multiplying the number of registered voters in the last preceding presidential election by the following amounts:

Position	Average amount per voter (cents)
Mayor	30
Members of the Board of Supervisors	12
Assessor, District Attorney, City Attorney, Sheriff, Treasurer, and Public Defender	8
Members of the Board of Education and the Board of Governors of the Community College District	5

For the 1973 election, by way of example, the maximum worked out to approximately $50,000 for a candidate for the Board of Supervisors, about half the amount spent in recent years by successful candidates.

Any excess collections had to be turned over to the General Fund of the City and County of San Francisco, and so did anonymous contributions beyond a total of $200 per candidate.

Additionally, the ordinance provided that any knowing or willful violation of the law was a misdemeanor punishable by a fine of at least $500. If a victorious candidate should be found guilty of violating the ordinance, the election would be void.

The new law presented three broad categories of accounting problems: (1) general problems of control inherent in any kind of accounting; (2) specific problems created by the peculiar requirements of the law; (3) problems raised by inadequacies in the law.

The first set of problems could hardly have been more basic. Such minimal system elements as double-entry recording, general ledgers, and subsidiary ledgers were infrequently used in prior campaigns. Thus, the volunteers framed the report and model system to make them accessible even to the uninitiated.

The unique features of the law called for a more sophisticated approach. Initially, the group assumed that expenses of fund-raising events would always exceed the 10 percent allowed by the law (and this proved invariably the case). Thus, revenue would be reduced by the 10

2. For example, if a fund-raising dinner grossed $1,000 and cost $250, only 10 percent of the $1,000, or $100, could be deducted; $900 would apply to the maximum aggregate contributions received, even though only $750 had been garnered. This formula encouraged campaigns to monitor their costs carefully.

percent and expense credited—in the cash receipts journal, assuring that the aggregate maximum contributions would be carefully watched. Actual expenses would then be charged against the same general ledger account, partially or fully offsetting the previous credit; this procedure allowed time to gather the data on expenses after the fund-raising event.

Because in-kind contributions had to be accounted for at their fair market value, sample general journal entries were included in the report to illustrate proper recording.

The ordinance required reporting of full details for each individual who contributed $50 or more to a campaign. Since individuals obviously could give more than once, subsidiary ledgers were essential to cumulate the total amount contributed through each reporting date. The same considerations applied to expenditures.

Although CSFN did not call on API to assess weaknesses in the law, some became obvious in the course of the assignment. The first was the absence of any de minimis provision regarding individual contributions or expenditures. Legally, every dime received for a cup of coffee at a coffee klatch and every quarter paid for a bumper sticker had to be recorded by donor; every telephone call and postage stamp had to be accounted for. To gather the name, address, employer, occupation, and place of business of each donor as the plate was being passed would have been laughable—even if it had been practicable. Therefore, the candidates had three choices: to ignore this aspect of the law, to decline this type of support, or to turn such unaccountable collections over to the general fund of the city.

Perhaps some limit (say $500, or 1 percent of total donations received) could have been placed on collections and disbursements of this sort, which need not be accounted for. Doing so would not only have relieved candidates and their treasurers of an undue burden but might also have prevented the more serious infractions of other aspects of the law that occur when people believe that compliance is so impractical as to be impossible.

Ambiguities and control difficulties arose in connection with the contributions by a candidate on his own behalf. The $2,500 maximum allowed to the candidate (including his immediate family) was plainly meant to cover the use of a personal auto and home telephone, as well as the rental value of an appropriate portion of the home, for campaign purposes. Because detecting and punishing such violations is virtually inconceivable, perhaps it would have been preferable either to exclude such expenses or to provide specific allowances for them. Once again, respect for the law also was at issue.

Although the law set out the deadlines for filing reports, it inexplicably neglected to specify the closing dates of the reporting periods. For example, for a November election, the first report might be due between October 11 and 15, but technically that report could have been in compliance with the law if it covered the period ending on June 30.

Finally, enforcement authority was confusingly divided between the Registrar of Voters and the District Attorney, and neither office was given supplemental appropriations to carry out their new responsibilities. Indeed, it was the failure of the registrar to provide forms and assistance to candidates that led to the request for help from San Francisco API.

Apart from the inadequacies of the law, the cost of obtaining copies of reports filed put citizens' groups and opposing candidates at a disadvantage. Since it was not uncommon for a candidate's report to contain 100 or more pages, and the registrar charged $.50 per page for copies, the report might cost $50 or more. Moreover, each of dozens of candidates for various offices in that first election filed at least three reports. Although the reports were available for inspection in the registrar's office, these costs seemed to limit its benefits to the very wealthy or the intensely interested (and more likely to those who were both).

API's report to the Coalition of San Francisco Neighborhoods included six proposed forms (reproduced at the end of this chapter). The report urged that the model "not be used blindly" and noted that it was not "the only system which would be adequate or acceptable. For example, some degree of automation in record-keeping and reporting might be economically desirable depending on the size, complexity and sophistication of the campaign." Furthermore, in keeping with its principle of avoiding competition with professional accounting firms—in fact, of encouraging their use for newly perceived needs—the report urged "that each campaign retain accounting consulting services to implement and supervise the . . . accounting system and its required controls." The system, or a suitable alternative, would lend itself "to independent verification should the campaign choose to utilize outside accounting services for this purpose."[3]

To complete its task, API held a series of seminars for campaign treasurers late in September. Notwithstanding wide media coverage of the report, the seminars were poorly attended. As one of the campaign treasurers expressed it, some were apparently concerned that questions asked in a group setting would provide clues to the strategy of the candidates. During the next few months, however, San Francisco API staff and volunteers on the case received numerous telephone questions relating to the report and to compliance with the law. Furthermore, one of the members of the Board of Supervisors wrote API that "I think the service you are performing is of inestimable value, and I want to congratulate you for your public interest in doing so."

3. All quotations in this paragraph are from the report to CSFN from API, September 6, 1973.

API's work on this matter plainly benefited the community. But beyond the special issue with which it was concerned, the case pointed to wider implications. Even more valuable assistance could be provided by professional accountants by involvement in developing the legislation itself and the control apparatus to make laws reasonable and enforceable.

Model Forms

EXHIBIT I

Campaign Chart of Accounts

Account Number	Account Name
101	Petty Cash
102	Cash in Bank
105	Pledges Receivable
110	Deposits
201	Payroll Taxes Withheld
300	Fund Balance
401	Contributions Received
405	Fund-Raising Events—Contributions Portion
405-1	Event A
405-2	Event B
405-3	Event C
410	Loans Received
415	Pledges Received
501	Referendum Costs
502	Printing Expense
503	Travel and Transportation Expense
505	Advertising Expense
505-1	Radio
505-2	Television
505-3	Newspaper & Periodicals
505-4	Billboards & Signs
505-5	Bumper Stickers, Buttons, Etc.
510	Postage
515	Telephone & Telegraph
520	Salaries
530	Office Supplies & Expenses
535	Rent
540	Consultants
545	Payroll Tax Expense
550	Miscellaneous Expense
560	Fund-Raising Events—Expense Portion
560-1	Event A
560-2	Event B
560-3	Event C

EXHIBIT II

General Journal—Sample Entries

		Debit	Credit
505-2	Advertising—Television	XX	
401	Contributions		XX
	To record television advertising donated by _____ at fair market value		
*105	Pledges Receivable	XX	
401	Contributions		XX
	To record contribution pledged by Mr. & Mrs. _____ to be paid on or before _____		

* (If the volume of pledges warrants, a separate "pledges journal" could be utilized.)

EXHIBIT III

Statement of Assets and Liabilities
November 7, 1973

Assets

Cash
Pledges Receivable
Deposits
    Total

Liabilities and Fund Balance

Liabilities—Payroll Taxes Withheld
Fund Balance
    Total

EXHIBIT IV

Statement of Receipts, Expenditures and Fund Balance
for the Periods Ended November 7, 1973

	October 25 to November 7, 1973	*September 1 (Inception) to November 7, 1973*
Receipts		
Contributions	_____	_____
Expenses		
Referendum Costs		
Fund-raising Costs		
Printing Expense		
Travel and Transportation Expense		
Advertising Expense		
Radio		
Television		
Newspapers & Periodicals		
Billboards & Signs		
Bumper Stickers, Buttons, Etc.		
Postage		
Telephone & Telegraph		
Salaries		
Office Supplies & Expenses		
Rent		
Consultants		
Payroll Tax Expense		
Miscellaneous Expense		
Total	_____	_____
Excess of Receipts over Expenses	_____	_____
Fund Balance—Beginning of Period		
Fund Balance—End of Period	_____	_____

EXHIBIT V

Candidate's Verification

I do hereby affirm that I have carefully reviewed for truthfulness and accuracy the financial statements of my campaign and of each committee subject to my control for the period September 1, 1973 to October 25, 1973 and at October 25, 1973 and that these statements, to my knowledge, are true and complete and meet the provisions of city and county of San Francisco Ordinance 261-73 dealing with campaign contributions and expenditures.

_____
Candidate

EXHIBIT VI

Campaign Treasurer's Verification

I do hereby verify that the accompanying campaign statements do in fact reflect all items of income, either received or pledged, and expenses paid directly or indirectly on behalf of the _____ campaign for the period September 1, 1973 to October 25, 1973 and its financial position at October 25, 1973. I certify that, to my knowledge, these statements are true and complete and meet the provisions of city and county of San Francisco Ordinance 261-73 dealing with campaign contributions and expenditures.

_____
Campaign Treasurer

___(7)___

The Expansion of San Francisco International Airport

For many years, officials of both the city and county of San Francisco desired to expand the facilities of the San Francisco International Airport to accommodate an expected growth in passenger traffic from about 14 million in 1971 to about 31 million by 1985. The city proposed a $390 million expansion project and suggested that it be financed by issuance of revenue bonds to avoid the necessity of taking the matter to the voters, as would be the case for general obligation bonds under California law.

The city's Airports Commission had original jurisdiction over the proposal, and held extensive hearings on it. Besides various city officials, the formidable proponents of the expansion program were the business community and organized labor. Business saw it as a major element in increasing tourism, one of the biggest industries in San Francisco, with a rippling effect beyond the direct beneficiaries such as hotels, restaurants, and entertainment facilities. Labor saw it as a much-needed opportunity for underemployed construction workers.

Against this array stood a number of environmental groups, which were asking some tough questions:

Why shouldn't the voters decide the issue?
Is the expansion really needed?
Is the projection of growth in passenger traffic reasonable?
Should some of the air traffic be diverted to other airports in the
    San Francisco Bay Area?
Will air and noise pollution worsen?
Can the feeder-road system handle the increase?
Will revenues be sufficient to pay off the bonds?
Who will be responsible for the bond payments if they are not?

One of the groups, the San Francisco Ecology Center, wrote to San Francisco Accountants for the Public Interest in April 1973, noting that though their "objections to this plan are obviously ecological in nature . . . its economic feasibility is also subject to serious question. Since, how-

71

ever, we lack the background necessary to render a reasonable judgment on this matter, we are seeking your help."

In accepting the assignment, the API executive committee deliberately left the scope of the engagement vague. Ordinarily, the committee specifically listed the issues they intended to investigate. In this complex case, with its massive accumulation of documents, however, merely identifying issues that could be analyzed within the limits of the available volunteer time and the specialized knowledge of the API team would have itself required inordinate time. Therefore, API agreed simply to be consultants to the center so that together they could gradually focus on those issues.

API had the unusual luxury of being under little pressure to complete the assignment. Hearings and pending law suits were expected to continue for at least a few years. However, as previous experience had taught, this was a mixed blessing. In the absence of an early deadline, significant progress on a case often was deferred, as later cases imposed "emergencies" and the human tendency to procrastinate asserted itself. To forestall this development, API's plan called for a series of reports on various phases of the case and a deadline for each.

All of the available documentary material was distributed to the team—a staff member and several volunteers—and then exchanged among them. In that way, everyone became familiar with the entire project even though each was concerned with only one element. During this process, the team met a number of times with the client, and attended various hearings before the city's Planning Commission, the Airports Commission, and the Finance Committee of the Board of Supervisors. They also sought information from the Federal Aviation Administration, the Civil Aeronautics Board, and state and regional planning and transportation agencies.

The principal document in the case was a report, "Financial Feasibility/Rates and Charges Analysis of the San Francisco International Airport Expansion Program," prepared by Peat, Marwick, Mitchell and Co. (Hereafter, this document will be referred to as the PMM report.) But if the PMM report was the most important document, it was far from the only one with which API had to deal. An Environmental Impact Report (EIR) was required by California law and an Environmental Impact Statement (EIS) was called for under federal law. Besides these, the Federal Aviation Administration requested an Environmental Impact Assessment Report (EIAR) as the preliminary to the EIS! The PMM report offers a forceful example of how a document prepared by a prestigious national firm can be selectively used to offer "cold facts."

API was concerned not so much with the validity or accuracy of the PMM report as with the significance of the limitations imposed on the work performed and with the political uses to which the report was being put.

First of all, as the report stated,

[PMM has been asked] to conduct financial feasibility rates and charges analyses to determine (1) the conditions under which the unfunded portions of the proposed Expansion Program could be financed by the sale of revenue bonds and (2) the rates and charges required from airline tenants and users to provide for continued self-sustaining fiscal operation of the Airport. This report is the product of these analyses; it includes a detailed financing plan documenting the required sale of additional bonds and . . . calculations of airline rates and charges (terminal building rental rates and landing fees) for Fiscal Year 1973-74 through 1984-85 required to support the Program.

In its introduction, the PMM report stated that "It should be noted that this report is not a statement of financial feasibility for the sale of revenue bonds."

The report then spelled out—in *seven* pages—the "key assumptions" on which the financial forecasts were based. These assumptions included, among other things, the timing and costs of construction, the timing and cost of bonds, the relation between the two, and the adjustability of rental revenues.

Further, the PMM report assumed that the 6 percent allowance for escalation of costs during the construction period was "reliable for the purposes of this analysis," and that the first increment of revenue bonds would be sold in the fall of 1973. The average inflation rate in the succeeding years has far exceeded that anticipated, and the first increment of revenue bonds still had not been sold two years after the date assumed.

In its conclusion the PMM report stated that "the purpose of this report has been to demonstrate that the implementation of the proposed San Francisco International Airport Expansion Program is financially viable *under certain conditions* [italics added]." It asserted that the expansion program "appears to be financially feasible" *if* average rates and charges to passengers, and the average user fee costs per enplaned passenger paid by airlines, were in line with those at other major airports; *if* the airlines supported the program; *if* the proposed agreement for adjusting landing fees indeed assured the cash flow to meet all airport requirements; and *if* the revenue bonds were sold.

Furthermore, all exhibits and schedules contained the footnote: "This statement has been prepared on the basis of the information and assumptions enumerated in the text. Because any forecast is subject to uncertainties, these forecasts are not represented as specific results which actually will be achieved."

In other words, the PMM report and the conclusions it offered were hedged by many qualifications, assumptions, disclaimers, and caveats, all carefully spelled out. In using,—or, more accurately, misusing—the report to usher the project through the political and bureaucratic decision-making processes, the proponents of the program ignored, misunderstood, or unintentionally misinterpreted these qualifications. The very title, casually read, seemed to imply that a national CPA firm had found the project financially feasible with no reservations.

The API reports were issued on May 21, 1973, October 26, 1973, and April 25, 1974. As the following extract from the May document shows, the questions API raised in the preliminary report fell into three main categories: the validity of the projections of airport use and revenues; the consideration of alternatives to the expansion program; and the staging of construction.

I) *Adequacy and accuracy of the projections of Peat, Marwick, Mitchell &*
   Co. (PMM) on revenues and expenditures
   (A) Because of agreement of the airlines to periodically (every three
       years) adjust landing fees under the so-called "break-even" policy
       [revenues budgeted to match expenses], PMM believes that adequate
       assurance of ability to meet expenses and bond amortization exists
       barring—
       1. A major national catastrophe
       2. An earthquake
   (B) Since landing fee adjustments are prospective only, insufficient con-
       sideration seems to have been given to financial problems which may
       arise within the three-year period.
   (C) A major miscalculation in the projections, particularly one with na-
       tional significance, could endanger the balance implicit in (A) above,
       with a cumulative and possible circular effect. For example in addi-
       tion to the possibilities indicated by PMM, the demonstrated vola-
       tility of the airline industry (evidenced by merger activity, corporate
       losses, defeat of the SST, and L.A.-type litigation), the energy crisis,
       and possible changes in traveling habits, could result in temporary
       or permanent effects on the figures. Should such changes be sig-
       nificant and require equally significant fare increases, travel would
       be discouraged, which would in turn reduce airline parking and con-
       cession income, again requiring increased fares . . . until a time
       when . . . a point of diminishing returns has been reached. At that
       stage, no further landing fee increases might be possible despite
       existing agreements and the SFIA would be in serious financial
       trouble. There would appear to be no alternative at that point for
       the City and County of San Francisco [than] to honor a non-legal
       commitment and cover shortages.
   (D) . . . A possible change in the existing federal law regarding federal
       non-taxability of revenue bond interest, . . . without compensating

subsidies, . . . could increase the cost of borrowing by approximately 40 percent and thus seriously affect the feasibility of the expansion.

(E) Parking revenue is a significantly greater percentage of total revenue than is the percentage of parking and related capital costs to total capital costs. A significant change in auto use could seriously affect the entire project. In addition, secondary effects and costs such as the Southern Crossing, Bayshore freeway widening, etc. should be considered in the total evaluation of this matter.

(F) We hope to examine and evaluate the models used by PMM in determining the estimated 31 million passenger usage of SFIA by 1985, particularly in view of the Airport Commission's 1970 projection that 24 million passengers would be using the SFIA in 1976 (now estimated by PMM for fiscal 1976 at 18.8 million or 22 percent less than the previous projection) and the conclusion of the Airport Commission Staff Report of December 1972 . . . "that the present $192 million Approved Expansion Program falls far short of satisfying the needs of the airport in the coming years; that there have been significant changes affecting many of the items included in that program since its approval in 1970." (p. 43)

(G) We hope to study and illustrate some of the possible fiscal implications of the failure to lease the 1,400,000 square feet of terminal space to the airlines at the projected rates, and to examine commitments by the airlines for such space.

(H) We plan to examine previous projections by staff and consultants in prior years and compare such projections to actual results.

(I) We plan to attempt to determine whether SFIA might face land acquisition suits similar to those of L. A. International Airport.

(J) Reference is made to the assumptions made by PMM in its report on pages 3 through 9, 24, 27, and 29, all of which qualify its conclusion as to financial feasibility.

II) *Alternatives Considered*

(A) PMM was not retained to deal with the question of which airport (San Jose or Oakland) should be expanded first. Thus, their report should in no way be considered an independent appraisal of the propriety or logic of spending $390 million to expand SFIA while Oakland's capacity can reportedly be increased from 2 to 12 million without significant capital costs.

(B) Although it is widely discussed in the industry, the problem of load factors below the 51 percent level are not discussed in the report. It would seem that major efforts should be made by airports, airlines and the CAB to substantially increase load factors to eliminate the pure waste represented by empty seats, prior to embarking on major expansion of existing facilities which would likely remain adequate for many years if aircraft were merely more fully utilized.

(C) In connection with the problem of auto congestion on Route 101, the EIR . . . notes that the airport "can encourage rescheduling of airline operations." This also has been widely discussed in the airline industry. We recognize that there are many problems involved with such rescheduling. However, it would seem that the time has long since come when airports around the country not merely encourage rescheduling of airline operations, but adamantly insist on such rescheduling. Coupled with reductions of fares for off peak hours, there can be little doubt that it is worth a major effort to determine whether present capacity could be increased dramatically (and airline profits increased perhaps even more dramatically) by encouraging flexible schedules and fares.

(D) . . . The EIR states:

"The estimated cost of this program is over $390 million. Several groups or individuals suggest that this money should be spent in other areas for the betterment of society. However, this money will be made available mainly through the sale of revenue bonds and the entire amount will be paid for by the users of the airport; hence, the money would not be available for other purposes."

This statement assumes that the $390 million exists in a vacuum. It does not. It would be represented by bonds purchased by individuals and institutions which could invest in other endeavours were this project not to exist. It would be paid for . . . by airlines and concessionaires who would otherwise have other uses for their money, and ultimately by airport customers or passengers who might prefer to spend their travel monies on wine, women, and song rather than half-empty aircraft and overbuilt and under-utilized airport facilities.

III) *Other Points*

(A) It is unclear at this point how the "staging" of this project would be controlled (other than by the periodic bond issues and the related feasibility reports required) to limit the construction should the passenger growth not meet expectations. There would appear to be a grave practical difficulty of halting the program once it is under way because of the interdependence of the construction and facilities, the momentum the project has as vested interests become committed to . . . major growth within its domain. Nonetheless, major emphasis should be placed on providing for public review of clearly planned stages so that the project might be stoppable before a BART-type financial problem can happen.

(B) There appears to be little reason that the repayment of the $24 million (in dollars worth far less than when the advances were made) by the airport to the City and County of San Francisco should not be accompanied by payment of a reasonable rate of interest on the unpaid balance from the time of such advances to the time of complete repayment.

(C) Cost-of-living escalation clauses of some commonly acceptable type should be standard for all airport leases. This has been common commercial practice even prior to the high present rate of inflation.

(D) Page 42 of the Airport Commission Staff Report of December 1972 states:

> "Any amendment to Section 6.408 of the City and County of San Francisco Charter that substantially changes the flow of Airport revenues will necessarily cause a reassessment of the financial feasibility of the program."

(E) That same page contains the following statement:

> "In order to insure that a major improvement program, such as is contemplated at San Francisco International Airport, is both prudent and financially feasible, the following conditions should be met: (1) each facility to be constructed should, at minimum, meet demonstrated requirements (public or tenant); (2) each facility or project should be economically justifiable; (3) the landing fee rates and rental rates required from tenant airlines to maintain, at a minimum, self-sufficient operation at the Airport both during and after completion of the Program should be reasonable; and (4) the tenant airlines should manifest their support and approval of the Program."

We question whether the PMM report and the EIR fully and adequately demonstrate that all of those conditions have been met. We further believe that alternate conditions and possibilities should be more thoroughly investigated and evaluated.

Not all of the questions raised in the first report were, in fact, investigated further. The Ecology Center and API agreed that given the potential results, some of them were not worth the time and effort required.

The second report, in late October, was considerably more focused.

We have examined the Peat, Marwick, Mitchell & Co. report and find that its projections as to garage revenues, passenger usage, space rental, and concessions are reasonable under current conditions and assumptions.

However, we are concerned with the reliance that can be placed on a forecast through 1985.

Long-term projections are inherently of limited dependability. This fact is expressed in an article in the January 1973 issue of *The Journal of Accountancy,* which reported that in England, where forecasts are subject to regulation, the law states: "Reporting accountants should not normally undertake to review and report on forecasts for more than the current accounting period, and provided a sufficiently significant part of the current year has elapsed, the next following accounting year." They continue that "The typical view of 'a sufficiently significant part of the current year' is six months and the maximum forward period is therefore eighteen months."

Under the current rules of the American Institute of CPAs, "A member or associate shall not permit his name to be used in conjunction with any forecast of the results of future transactions in a manner which may lead to the belief that the member or associate vouches for the accuracy of the forecast."

When a CPA associates himself with a forecast, a full disclosure must be made of the major assumptions made in the preparation of the statements. Some of the assumptions made by PMM are enumerated in part below.

1. The cost estimates for the Airport Expansion Program developed by W. J. Nicholson Co. with the assistance of MDA Construction Cost Consultants are reliable.

2. The remaining $31.9 million of general obligation bonds will be sold and will have a net interest cost of 6 percent.

3. All revenue bonds sold will have a net interest cost of 7 percent.

4. Rental rates will be adjusted annually to meet revenue requirements.

5. The construction schedule provided by Bechtel, Inc. can be used to determine the timing of funds.

6. Cost of utilities sold is projected at constant annual percentage increases and then a $500,000 constant "gross margin" is assumed to project gross revenue from the sale of utilities.

＊   ＊   ＊

Available, actual data compared with projections by PMM for fiscal 1973 are shown below:

	*Projected**	*Actual*
Passenger Usage	15,320,000	15,208,000
Garage Revenue (Total)	$3,900,000	$4,000,000
Garage Revenue (per Enplaned Passenger)	$0.50	$0.53

* This projection was based on six months of actual data and six months of forecasted results.

We believe that the *Summary of Annual Debt Service Requirements* prepared by PMM is misleading in that it does not disclose the cost of the debt service by year through to maturity.

Although garage revenues in fiscal year 1973 exceeded the PMM projections, certain factors may severely restrict such revenues in the future. The Airport Commission has assured Peninsula residents that BART will absorb the additional travelers to and from the airport. The EIR estimates "27.5 percent–32.5 percent of airline passengers will use BART," while the PMM projection considers only the current 15 percent mass transit usage rate. . . .

Recently announced EPA-proposed curbs on gasoline and parking facilities will likely take their toll on garage needs. For these reasons, we believe that the $53,500,000 garage expansion project should be given a lower priority in the proposed expansion program.

We have reviewed the projected landing fees and find that they are reasonable considering what the airlines already pay in many foreign airports and that landing fees are not a material portion of the cost of air travel to individual passengers.

One of the assumptions used in the PMM financial feasibility study is a 100 percent occupancy factor for the rentable terminal space allotted to the airlines. The exhibit attached (p. 80) demonstrates the loss of revenue resulting from occupancy factors of 80, 90, and 95 percent and the necessary increase in rental rates to arrive at the required revenue.

Assuming that the airlines will absorb any increase in rental rates necessitated by lower occupancy factors, the airport and the City of San Francisco would not suffer any losses. However, should the airlines discontinue their full financial support of the airport by refusing to agree to periodic increases in rental rates and landing fees, any losses incurred by the airport would have a direct effect upon the repayment of the City's loan to the airport. The PMM study presented the expenses of the airport in the order of priority of payment. At the bottom of the list is payment to the City for funds advanced to the airport by the City prior to 1957. Any losses up to $2,000,000 will therefore apparently have to be absorbed by the projected payments to the City.

Certain modifications to the operational patterns at the airport might lead to more efficient use of plant investment. Under current operating patterns, port locations are assigned to airlines on an exclusive basis and at each airline's choice of airport. This type of assignment results in a need for a larger number of port facilities than if the ports were used by the carrier only during the period of time needed by that carrier, thus freeing the port for use by other carriers during other periods. The determining factor in calculating expansion needs is the method used to decide the determined number of port facilities and in turn the number of operations to be incurred within a set time frame. The facilities under consideration are designed to handle a pattern of usage which is set to minimize the airline capital investment requirements and not the City's, namely a greater number of ports at the SFIA in the face of low usage rates throughout the Bay area. It would appear that the City should examine these airline operating patterns.

In the absence of rerouting of flights to under-utilized neighboring airports, it is apparent that some expansion of SFIA will be needed to accommodate future increases in passenger traffic. The question, therefore, is not expansion itself, but rather how much. There is not yet a consensus as to whether the expansion project is too ambitious, or, for that matter, too conservative. Therefore, staging or phasing of the construction appears to be the viable financial alternative. The question of whether or not the project could be halted if it were determined that no more expansion was necessary was brought up in the EIR, Volume II, pages 4–14.

"Q. Is a smaller project feasible? What would be the effect of no expansion?
"A. Although this project is large, it is going to be built in phases, sequentially. The construction can be delayed between phases, if this is found desirable by the Commission."

The reply is plainly inadequate. There would appear to be a grave practical difficulty of halting the program once it is under way because of the

San Francisco International Airport Revenue Loss and Rate Increases at Varying Levels of Occupancy

Year	Average Rentable Square Feet	Required Revenue	Required Average Airline Rental Rates (100% Occupancy)	Loss in Revenue If Occupancy Factor Decreases			Increase in Required Airline Rental Rate to Compensate for Loss of Revenue Incurred by Lower Occupancy Factor		
				by 5%	by 10%	by 20%	95%	90%	80%
1973/74	395,000	$ 4,670,000	$11.35	$234,000	$ 467,000	$ 934,000	$0.62	$1.31	$2.95
1974/75	420,000	$ 5,030,000	$12.00	$252,000	$ 503,000	$1,006,000	$0.63	$1.33	$2.99
1975/76	850,000	$ 8,600,000	$10.10	$430,000	$ 860,000	$1,720,000	$0.53	$1.12	$2.53
1976/77	1,085,000	$10,230,000	$ 9.45	$512,000	$1,023,000	$2,046,000	$0.50	$1.05	$2.36
1977/78	1,180,000	$16,650,000	$14.10	$833,000	$1,665,000	$3,330,000	$0.64	$1.49	$3.53
1978/79	1,265,000	$13,190,000	$14.40	$910,000	$1,819,000	$3,638,000	$0.76	$1.60	$3.60
1979/80	1,285,000	$13,440,000	$14.35	$922,000	$1,844,000	$3,688,000	$0.76	$1.59	$3.59
1980/81	1,335,000	$18,640,000	$14.00	$932,000	$1,864,000	$3,728,000	$0.74	$1.56	$3.50
1981/82	1,385,000	$18,740,000	$13.50	$937,000	$1,874,000	$3,748,000	$0.71	$1.50	$3.38
1982/83	1,400,000	$18,640,000	$13.30	$932,000	$1,864,000	$3,728,000	$0.70	$1.48	$3.33
1983/84	1,400,000	$18,350,000	$13.10	$916,000	$1,835,000	$3,670,000	$0.69	$1.46	$3.27
1984/85	1,400,000	$17,570,000	$12.55	$878,000	$1,757,000	$3,514,000	$0.66	$1.40	$3.14

interdependence of the construction and facilities, and the momentum of the project as vested interests become committed to its completion. Moreover, any arbitrary cut-off of funds for construction could have adverse and uneconomical consequences for the airport projects that are partially complete. As it is, it does not appear that the proposed construction program is organized to allow for premature termination.

A staged plan of construction, subject to review and stoppable at certain predetermined points, would provide a failsafe mechanism for unwarranted expansion without undesirable side effects.

We feel that staging is essential because, in this era of accelerated change, factors which few of us were even aware of a year ago . . . now demand major consideration. . . . They include imminent fuel and power limitations, decreasing population growth rates, and stricter environmental controls. This is exemplified by the October 19, 1973 agreement by three major airlines to reduce the number of flights in and out of San Francisco, purportedly due to fuel shortages. Achieving reliable projections for revenues, expenses, construction costs, population and passenger traffic over a twelve-year period is extremely difficult. A device is needed that would allow for major revisions in construction plans—whether it be for a greater or lesser expansion—on a periodic basis. Since the landing fees are to be renegotiated with the airlines every three years, the stages could be planned to coincide with the renegotiation proceedings. The expansion project could be evaluated in light of then current projections; the airlines' willingness to pay for future expansion made subject to public review; and the project redesigned if necessary.

The third and final report, in April 1974, attempted to evaluate some of the weaknesses of the model that generated the forecasted level of the airport operations, which API believed had received insufficient attention in public discussions of the project. The report stated:

Overall Characteristics

Two of the general characteristics of the growth model are that it yields an essentially linear result, and that it is unconstrained. Neither of these characteristics is descriptive of the historic pattern of growth at the airport.

During the period 1950–68, growth occurred at an increasing rate. Graphically, this pattern is characterized by a curve with an increasing rather than constant slope upwards. (See Exhibit A.) In the four years 1969–72 passenger usage leveled out between 13,500,000 and 13,900,000 passengers a year. While this period can be characterized as linear, it does not support the projection of a doubling of usage in the succeeding eleven years. Over the entire projection period, a pattern of constant growth in number of passengers, and therefore a . . . decreasing rate of growth, does not accurately reflect the historical growth pattern. A linear growth pattern applied to the projection may not therefore be appropriate to the staged expansion plan contemplated at San Francisco International Airport.

A leveling of usage after a period of rapid growth may indicate a con-

straint in total achievable usage. While we are not prepared to determine
which variable caused the constraint, we do know that it is not airport size,
because airport usage increased in 1973 without expansion. The airport still
has unused capacity today, as evidenced by Peat, Marwick, Mitchell & Co.'s
1974 estimated usage of 16,460,000 passengers. The model does not provide
for a constraint of the magnitude which occurred during the four years ending
in 1972.

While lack of constraint does not invalidate the model, it could involve
some degree of distortion. The question then becomes the degree of distortion
of the model over a thirteen-year period. When it is considered that parking
revenue, which is directly related to airport usage, is estimated to reach
$11,000,000 annually by 1985, an error of 10 percent would cause a $1,100,000
variance in revenue in that year.

Sensitivity of Variables

Responding to questions about the achievability of 31,000,000 passengers if
population were held constant, the EIR . . . states that if employment and
total personal income increase 30 percent there will be no problem in achieving
the projected results. It is unclear exactly what was meant by that statement,
but the EIR must be referring to annual increases because the projected annual
5 percent increase in total income over thirteen years results in a compounded
growth of 88.6 percent over the base. It is unrealistic to assume a substantial
annual employment increase when population is being held constant and
absurd to contemplate 30 percent increases in personal income except during
periods of major economic upheaval.

The EIR states that, regardless of what happens to the Bay area, the
biggest contributing factor to increased passenger usage is the nonresident
visitor. While it is true that 40 percent of the passengers using the San
Francisco airport are not residents of the Bay area, the forecasting model does
not include any non-resident variables which would give an indication of the
status of the national economy and thus the non-residents' ability to travel.

Personal Income

Analysis of the ABAG forecasting model also shows that zero growth in total
personal income would yield no appreciable increase in passenger usage between 1973 and 1985. According to the model, personal income is the only
variable which, if held constant, could hold usage constant.

In forecasting growth, the model assumes a 5 percent annual growth rate
in total personal income. Personal income growth is a function of both economic growth (per capita income) and population growth. In the period
1940–72, per capita income rose at a rate of only 2.8 percent per annum.
Total personal income has grown at a rate of 4.5 percent but was assisted by
a sizeable growth in population. Current Census Bureau reports show that
population growth has slowed, especially in the metropolitan areas of over
2,000,000 in population, where practically no growth has occurred from 1970

to 1972. The Census Bureau now predicts only a 3.1 percent growth for the Bay area for the years 1970 to 1975, which would result in a population of 4.3 million by 1975, the point at which the model is using 5.0 million.

Such a decrease in the projected population is a reason to question whether total personal income should be estimated to increase at a rate of less than 5 percent per year. If all other variables except population and personal income are taken at the projected level, airport traffic would be 24.3 million in fiscal 1985. Usage would then be 22 percent less than forecast.

This report has been prepared on the basis of the information and assumptions delineated in the text. Because all forecasts are subject to uncertainties, we do not represent any forecasts as specific results which will actually be achieved.

EXHIBIT A

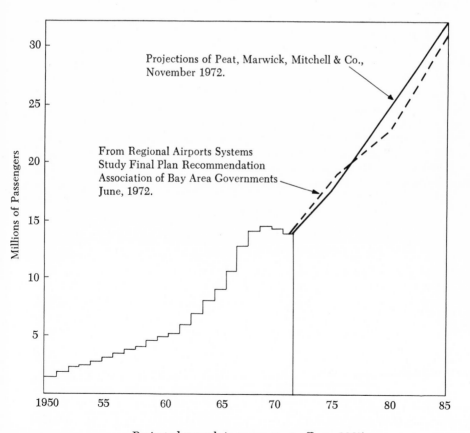

Projected growth in passenger traffic to 1985

Client Evaluation Letters

SF API received two evaluation letters from its client on this case. The first, dated February 8, 1974, stated:

The Board of Directors, staff and membership of the San Francisco Ecology Center would like to express their sincere appreciation for the prompt and excellent service which API has provided to assist us in analyzing the economic and forecasting aspects of the [San Francisco International Airport] Expansion Program.

[API's] professional accounting assistance, in our opinion, was an invaluable aid in our campaign which questioned the economic and environmental impacts which the sponsors of the expansion claim will result from the expansion. . . . We feel that the report was instrumental in changing the mind of certain elected officials who at one time supported the expansion. . . .

The qualifying language (concerning fuel shortage, etc.) in API's most recent opinion letter on the air travel growth predictions by Airport management has now become a matter of reality with a substantial impact on these predictions.

The second letter, received in late June 1974, added to this assessment:

The third, and final, API report on the Expansion Program which we recently received has been invaluable. . . . API's evaluation of the characteristics of the growth model used by airport management to formulate predictions of air travel growth at San Francisco International Airport has been very persuasive to various planners. As with the first two reports, it is the objectivity and professionalism inherent in the reports which add immeasurably to the strength of the positions and arguments we have advanced.

Conclusion

At the end of 1975, the expansion program had not received final approval. The proposal has been heard and reheard before countless agencies, commissions, committees, boards, and councils. City, county, state, and national governments have been involved. And, if all that were not enough, the issue is muddied by a jurisdictional dispute between San Francisco, which owns the land on which the airport stands, and San Mateo County (just south of San Francisco), where it is located. Many San Mateo County residents strongly oppose the expansion because it might aggravate pollution and congestion; but the law is unclear concerning the control which the county may exercise over the facility. In addition, several law suits were filed to stop or delay the project. One was appealed, and new suits have been threatened. The legal cloud has effectively deferred the approval and marketing of the revenue bonds.

Time usually works on the side of bureaucracy in a dispute with the public because it has the staying power and the patience to let the opposition burn itself out, but this case is an exception. The opposition has grown to include two national environmental organizations, the Sierra Club and Friends of the Earth (both of which maintain their head offices in San Francisco), along with the Ecology Center and San Francisco Tomorrow. Successes in delaying the project have mobilized the opposition of individual citizens in San Mateo County, and many San Franciscans are taking a second look at the expansion program because of financial problems that have beset other projects that have been financed, sponsored, or promoted by the city.

Events have not been kind to the proponents of the expansion program. Fortunately, the assumption in the PMM report that there would be no major national catastrophe or an earthquake has not been contradicted. But:

— The 6 percent allowance for inflation of costs has proven to be only half that which occurred in the following year.
— Estimated costs now stand at $469 million, a $79 million increase. This was caused by inflation-related increases of $115 million which were partially offset by the deletion of $36 million worth of improvements.
— The growth rate of air travel has leveled off, raising further questions about the accuracy of projected needs.
— Several major airlines have suffered massive financial problems. The inability of even one major carrier to meet its obligations to pay landing fees and rent would destroy the ability of the airport to pay off the revenue bonds as scheduled.
— The municipal bond market is plagued with uncertainty and instability. This condition is due partially to the fiscal crisis facing New York City, but also involves historically high interest rates. The 7 percent projected rate for revenue bonds now appears to be too low. The rate at which the bonds could be sold at this date would be much closer to 8 percent, causing further havoc with the cash flow. In any case, by late 1975, the first increment of revenue bonds had yet to be sold, though the assumption was that they would be out in the fall of 1973.

The expansion program may or may not be completed in its present form. There are sound reasons for and against the project, and they have been articulated and supported by professionals from many disciplines. At the least, the final decision will have been made after full and open discussion, participation, and representation by all of the parties interested in this complex policy dispute.

___(8)___

Financial Analysis of a Community College District

The Peralta Community College District in California was established on November 19, 1963, by the voters of the six East Bay cities of Albany, Berkeley, Emeryville, Oakland, Piedmont, and Alameda. Its aim was to operate a junior college system of education starting July 1, 1964. The District came into being without owning any permanent facilities or campus sites, and at first it utilized the Laney and Merritt campuses which were the property of the Oakland Unified School District and were leased at an annual cost in excess of $600,000. The trustees decided that several college campuses, located in different geographical areas, would best serve the needs of Peralta District.

After an investigation regarding site location, capital construction, and financing for permanent college campuses for the constituency of the district, the trustees decided to construct and operate four full scale degree-granting colleges; in the Berkeley-Albany-Emeryville area (the North Peralta section of the district); in the East Oakland hills; in the center of Oakland; and in Alameda. The funds for these activities were to come from the sale by the district of $47,000,000 in general obligation bonds.

Subsequent to the passage of the bond measure by the voters, the district began to expend monies from these designated funds for construction of new campuses at all of the sites except for the Berkeley-Albany-Emeryville area.

In 1966, contrary to the recommendation of a site-selection committee, the trustees refused to retain the current site of North Peralta College, a junior college, as the new fourth campus for the Berkeley-Albany-Emeryville area, and subsequently announced their intention to phase out that college. Then, in the spring of 1975, the trustees proposed to build the Berkeley Learning Pavilion, which drew criticism as a "glorified adult school" which would not fulfill the representations of the district that "all colleges within the system would be comprehensive Community Colleges offering, to a broad spectrum of students, a varied program of courses in university transfer fields, trade and technical occupations, business and semi-professional areas and general education."

86

On February 7, 1967, the district entered into an agreement which, as of July 1, 1968, annexed the Plumas Unified School District to the Peralta Community College District. This annexation brought into the district Feather River College, which is approximately 250 miles away from the district's main geographical area.

The Associated Students of North Peralta College complained because it seemed that none of the bond money had been allocated toward the building of a new campus in their area. Alleging that this was contrary to the original intent and representations of the district, they sought help from the Legal Aid Society of Alameda County.

API Steps In

On August 29, 1973, Legal Aid requested the assistance of San Francisco Accountants for the Public Interest in extracting information from the accounting records of the District to aid the students in evaluating the legal alternatives. The letter pointed out that

[the Peralta] community consists largely of low-income minority people who depend on this college to provide skills and services needed for their livelihood. . . .

Now, eight years [after the bond issue], this money has largely been spent on three colleges in the southern part of the District, and the Peralta District has taken on another college in Quincy, California [Feather River], without consulting the Alameda County taxpayers. The residents of the northern part of the district, Albany, Berkeley, Emeryville and North Oakland are served by the North Peralta Community College on Grove Street, which is not staffed, funded, or equipped on a comparable level with its sister Peralta Colleges of Laney, Merritt, Alameda, or Feather River.

Noting that drastic reductions in the college's operations had made it impossible for students to complete their required courses of study there, Legal Aid suggested an examination of funding policies and expenditures to see whether the taxpayers' funds were being "reasonably spent." Legal Aid sought API's help in answering the following questions:

1. How was the 1965 bond money (and matching funds attracted by it) spent, what remains of this money, and, if any, what is it slated for?
2. What share of the original bond money was allocated to the north district college, versus what has actually been spent on the college serving this community population?
3. What share was spent on Feather River College, 250 miles away,

which was taken on by Peralta *after* the bond issue was passed, and not included in it, and how much other money has been spent on Feather River College?

4. On what basis were funds for the 1972–73, and 1973–74 budgets allocated, and did NPCC receive an equitable share of funds based on this? How much will Feather River get for 1973–74?

5. What federal funding was NPCC eligible for, what was received, and how was it spent?

API promptly reviewed the case. Plainly, it met the criteria: the Legal Aid Society was a nonprofit tax-exempt organization; neither it nor the student association could afford the accounting services they sought in pressing their case; and the issue turned on complex financing and accounting matters that, without API's assistance, might be obscured or, at best, incompletely presented. On September 7, API agreed to take the case.

Because the assistance requested by the client entailed access to certain internal accounting records, the cooperation of the District was essential. The Vice Chancellor of Business for the District granted this access and throughout the field work the district was helpful in supplying information, working space, and staff assistance.

To estimate how many hours would be needed to extract the required information, approximately three days were spent with District accounting personnel reviewing the accounting records and financial reports to determine how the proceeds from the bond sales were accounted for, the types of information generated by their basic accounting system, and the system used to account for campus construction costs. Also discussed were internal controls, the availability of supporting documentation, and the degree of compliance with certain generally accepted accounting principles.

The nature of the case and the need to perform most of the work at the District's offices dictated that the matter be assigned to a single volunteer. His selection was based on his knowledge and experience in fund accounting, his availability, and his interest in the case. During the field work, district officials were kept fully informed. Problem areas, assumptions, and conclusions were discussed with District accounting personnel, and their opinions were solicited. Their familiarity with the accounting system made this practice useful as well as courteous. Formal workpapers were prepared and assembled for permanent maintenance; these supported all financial data, representations, and conclusions presented in SF API's final report.

After completion of the field work certain steps were taken to assure a report that could be understood by the client and that contained no errors, significant omissions, or comments that were not responsive to the client's inquiry.

All workpapers supporting the report were reviewed by another SF API volunteer. The report draft was reviewed by SF API's executive director, by each member of SF API's executive committee, and by district personnel to identify any factual errors. And finally, the report draft was circulated to the client and the attorneys participating in the case to elicit their comments.

Approximately one year after the acceptance of the case, the following report was issued:

As requested by Legal Aid Society of Alameda County we have extracted from the accounting records of the Peralta Community College District information in response to inquiries indicated in our letter of arrangement dated September 7, 1973.

In this connection certain statements and schedules of financial data have been prepared which summarize this information regarding the Peralta Community College District. We have also prepared responses to your inquiries which include our interpretation of the data presented and other comments which we feel will assist you. (See attachment)

These statements and schedules which include the plant funds balance sheets as of June 30, 1974 and a statement of changes in plant funds balances for the nine fiscal years then ended do not purport to present the financial position and the results of operations for the Peralta Community College District as a whole. The data presented in these statements, schedules and response to your inquiries were not audited by Accountants for the Public Interest nor was there performed any study and evaluation of the existing internal control as a basis for reliance thereon. Accordingly, we do not express an opinion as to whether these statements, schedules and responses to your inquiries fairly present the data reflected therein nor the extent to which they comply with generally accepted accounting principles.

This information was gathered to assist the Associated Students of North Peralta Community College in evaluating their legal alternatives in connection with a continuing dispute as to equitable allocation of bond revenue and general purpose funds among the individual colleges within the district.

Our services are available to the extent necessary regarding any clarification, follow-up or further analysis concerning the data submitted.

Attachment to Letter Dated September 27, 1974
 Response to Inquiries from Legal Aid Society of Alameda County

The following represents a guide to the attached statements and schedules and our interpretation of the data presented therein:

1. *How the 1965 bond monies and matching funds attracted by it were spent, what remains of this money, if any, and what it is slated for.*

During the period beginning in April 1966 and ending in October 1968 the Peralta Community College District received $47,000,000 from the sale of bonds which were approved by the voters of Alameda County in 1965. Schedule II indicates that these funds were deposited in a County Treasury account which had been designated to be used solely for capital outlay purposes. Other funds totalling $12,473,931 for the nine years ended June 30, 1974 were also deposited in this account and were also designated for capital outlay purposes. District warrants (i.e. checks) were then drawn upon this cash account to pay for various capital improvements as costs were incurred. Because of the combining of all funds into one County Treasury cash account, a precise identification of specific capital expenditures with bond money, as distinguished from other monies received, is not possible, nor can there be an accurate statement of what portion, if any, of the ending balance at June 30, 1974 represents original bond monies or other monies received. The most significant transactions during this nine-year period were the purchase and improvement of college land sites and the construction of college campuses in Alameda, Oakland Civic Center area, and the Oakland Hills area.

The attached statements supply the following information:

During the nine years ended June 30, 1974 the above-mentioned monies designated for capital outlay were increased by the following revenue (Schedule II):

Sale of bonds		$47,000,000
Federal and State grants	$4,143,115	
Interest on investments	327,973	
Transfers from general fund		
of net restricted tax revenues	6,543,222	
Transfers from other plant funds	1,438,829	
Other	20,792	
		12,473,931
		$59,473,931

During this same nine year period this fund was reduced by the following expenditures (Schedule II):

Purchase and improvement of land sites	$13,805,300
Building construction	40,062,521
Other expenditures	3,246,382
	$57,114,203

In connection with costs of construction data for each school, the District, during the period 1966–1973, maintained a record which accumulated expenditures for campus construction by individual school. This record accumulated the construction expenditures which were made from all funds, including capital expenditures from the general fund. This record indicated that the

District, as a whole, from all funds, spent $3,699,154, $10,589,100 and $43,281,632 on sites, site improvements, and buildings, respectively, during the eight fiscal years ended June 30, 1973 (Schedule III). Of this total of $57,569,886 expended for capital outlay, the individual schools participated in the following approximate percentages (Schedule III):

Merritt College	26.70%
Laney College	47.27
College of Alameda	21.05
North Peralta College:	
improvement of portable buildings	.05
cost associated with Berkeley-Albany site selection	.07
Feather River College	.43
Oakland Airport	.02
Warehouse Relocation	.02
	95.61%

In the opinion of District Management the internal accounting control surrounding the maintenance of this record was inadequate and, as a result, the total of the above percentages does not equal 100% because the record totals do not agree with total capital expenditures as reflected on the annual financial statements.

At June 30, 1974 the fund designated for capital outlay which received the $47,000,000 bond revenue (plus other revenue) had assets of $2,497,263 composed of cash and amounts due from general purpose funds of $1,432,639, and $1,064,624, respectively. This fund owed $248,703 in general liabilities at June 30, 1974. The net balance of this fund, assets minus liabilities, equals $2,248,560 at June 30, 1974. Of this total the Board of Trustees has reserved $500,000 for acquisition of a site for relocation of North Peralta College. The remainder of this net balance may be used for any major building programs conducted by the District (Schedule I).

District officials indicated their belief that this $2,248,560 is what remains of federal and state grants and is therefore committed to those unfinished projects for which the grants were received. At June 30, 1974 there were no construction projects in progress which were funded by the federal government.

The following are state-funded construction projects which are in progress at June 30, 1974:

1. Laney Theater
2. Merritt Library
3. College of Alameda Gymnasium/Locker Building
4. Feather River Maintenance/Warehouse Building
5. Merritt Swimming Pool
6. Merritt Outdoor Physical Education Facilities
7. College of Alameda Library

At June 30, 1974, costs to complete these projects are estimated by the District to total $10,727,832. Anticipated additional revenues to be received under state grants for reimbursement of future costs equal $9,911,185. This data indicates that all but $816,647 in future construction costs under government financed projects will be paid for by money which will be received in the future as costs are incurred. In any case, as we have stated above, the District's method of accounting does not provide a means by which anyone can attribute the original source of the remaining fund balance.

The District has two other funds from which capital outlays are made. The Education Code provides that a portion of non-resident tuition be recorded in Special Reserve Fund No. 1 and used only for capital outlay purposes. Amounts in the fund from other sources may be used for general purposes. At June 30, 1974 this fund had a net remaining balance of $556,044. Special Reserve Fund No. 2 has been designated by the Board of Trustees for capital outlay relating to community services. Unexpended community services override taxes are transferred to this fund. The Education Code provides that such funds may be expended only for community services purposes. At June 30, 1974 this fund had a net remaining balance of $1,016,009.

2. *What share of the original bond money was allocated to the North District College, versus what has actually been spent on the College serving this community population?*

Based on assumptions underlying the computation of the 1965 bond requirements and the average daily attendance at the North Peralta College had that college been operating independently in 1965 as it does presently, there would have been allocated approximately $4,000,000 for building construction costs, plus land purchases and improvement costs (Schedule VI).

The District's accounting records indicate that a total of approximately $70,000 has been spent specifically for capital outlay during the period 1966 through 1973 of which $43,000 represented consultant fees in connection with the selection of a site in the Berkeley-Albany area.

3. *What share was spent on Feather River College, 250 miles away, which was taken on by the District after the bond issue was passed and not included in it, and how much other money has been spent on Feather River College?*

As mentioned in 1. above the commingling of bond sales revenue with other revenues prevents an accurate statement as to what portion of the $47,000,000 was spent on Feather River College. However, of all District capital expenditures for the period 1966–1973 approximately $245,000 was spent on Feather River College (Schedule III).

As to the general expenditures during the period 1968–1974 the District has spent approximately $6,700,000 (includes pro rata cost of district administration—Note 8 to statements and schedules) on behalf of Feather River College which is approximately $1,900,000 in excess of revenues produced by the operation of the College (Schedule V).

4. *On what basis were funds for the 1972–73, and 1973–74 budgets allocated, and did NPCC receive an equitable share of funds based on this? How much will Feather River get for 1973–74?*

The procedure by which the District's annual general purpose budget is prepared is stated briefly as follows:

A Budget Committee composed of two representatives from each college, one representative for classified personnel, and the Vice Chancellor of Administrative and Business Services develops the budget:

1. Based on ending account balances, anticipated revenues, and necessary ending balances the Budget Committee determines the amount of general purpose funds available during the up-coming budget year.
2. From these general purpose funds available, deductions are made for teacher salaries and expenditures allocable to the District as a whole, such as expenses resulting from the operation of District offices, District insurance, fringe benefits, etc.
3. What monies remain, or discretionary funds, are allocated to the five individual schools based on estimated average daily attendance (A.D.A.). These discretionary funds are used to pay such school expenses as building operation and maintenance, supplies, etc.
4. After receiving these budget allocations of discretionary funds, the individual schools then prepare statements indicating how they plan to spend this money.
5. The Board of Trustees has final approval authority for the overall District budget.

As to the question of whether NPCC received an equitable share of funds and what portion was received by Feather River in 1973–74, reference is made to Schedule IV. It is noted that this schedule is to be reviewed taking into consideration that certain costs will be incurred which are not strictly related to student attendance. Irrespective of how many students are attending the school, if the school is open there are certain fixed costs which will be incurred. These fixed costs have not been excluded from those expenditures presented in Schedule IV. The fact that these costs are included results in larger expenditures per A.D.A. for the schools with small A.D.A.

5. *What federal monies did North Peralta Community College receive, and how was it spent?*

During the nine years ended June 30, 1974 $4,641,715 was recorded as Capital Fund revenue from various federal and state grants. Discussions with District Management indicate that none of these funds were received for construction projects at North Peralta Community College (Schedule VII). These discussions also indicated that because the land upon which North Peralta is located is not owned by the District, state funding under the Junior College Construction Act (Stern Act) is not available.

The accompanying statements and schedules listed below were not audited by us, and accordingly we do not express an opinion on them.

Schedule	*Title*	*Period*
I.	Plant Funds Balance Sheet	June 30, 1974
II.	Statements of Changes in Plant Funds Balances	For the nine fiscal years ended June 30, 1974
III.	Statement of Capital Expenditures By School	For the eight fiscal years ended June 30, 1973
IV.	Statement of General Purpose Expenditures Per A.D.A. By School	For each of the fiscal years ended June 30, 1971, 1972, 1973 and 1974
V.	Statement of General Purpose Revenue and Expenditures for Feather River College	For the six fiscal years ended June 30, 1974
VI.	Statement of Assumptions Underlying Computation of 1965 Bond Requirements	N/A
VII.	Statement of Federal and State Grant Revenue	For the nine fiscal years ended June 30, 1974

SCHEDULE I

Peralta Community College District
Plant Funds Balance Sheets

June 30, 1974
(Unaudited)

	Unexpended Plant Funds (Capital Outlay)			
	Total	*Capital*	*Special Reserve #1*	*Special Reserve #2*
Assets				
Cash	$1,766,634	$1,432,639	$ 97,408	$ 236,587
Investments in U.S. Bonds	860,000	–	290,000	570,000
Due from Current unrestricted funds	1,442,682	1,064,624	168,636	209,422
Total	$4,069,316	$2,497,263	$556,044	$1,016,009
Liabilities and Funds Balances				
Liabilities:				
Accounts payable	$ 248,703	$ 248,703	$ –	$ –
Total	248,703	248,703	–	–
Funds Balances:	3,820,613	2,248,560	556,044	1,016,009
Total	$4,069,316	$2,497,263	$556,044	$1,016,009

The accompanying notes are an integral part of these statements and schedules.

SCHEDULE II

Peralta Community College District
Statement of Changes in Plant Funds Balances
for the Nine Fiscal Years Ended June 30, 1974

(Unaudited)

	Total	Capital Fund	Special Reserve Fund No. 1	Special Reserve Fund No. 2	(Note 3) Student Center Construction Funds
Revenues					
Proceeds from bond sales	$48,300,000	$47,000,000	$	$	$1,300,000
Federal and state grants	4,288,115	4,143,115	145,000		
Junior College tax relief grants	241,803		241,803		
Non-resident junior college tuition tax	103,736		103,736		
Tuition from other junior college districts	227,239		227,239		
Interest on investments	1,582,333	327,973	948,007	306,353	
Entitlement under Junior College Construction Act of 1965	353,600		353,600		
Rentals and leases	19,783	19,783			
Sales of land and buildings	37,920		37,920		
Other	1,009	1,009			
	55,155,538	51,491,880	2,057,305	306,353	1,300,000

SCHEDULE II—Continued

	Total	Capital Fund	Special Reserve Fund No. 1	Special Reserve Fund No. 2	(Note 3) Student Center Construction Funds
Expenditures					
Campus construction costs for the eight fiscal years ended June 30, 1973: (Note 3)					
Sites	3,608,386	3,608,386			
Site improvements	10,573,900	10,045,368		338,813	189,719
Buildings	42,984,749	38,243,684		889,587	3,851,478
	57,167,035	51,897,438		1,228,400	4,041,197
Campus construction costs for the fiscal year ended June 30, 1974: (Note 3)					
Sites	4,600	4,600			
Site improvements	146,946	146,946			
Buildings	1,818,837	1,818,837			
Equipment (Note 3)	2,930,928	2,884,709		46,219	
Redemption of street improvement bonds of 1968	320,000	320,000			
Bond interest paid and matured bond interest coupons	15,840	15,840			
Replacement of equipment	9,827	9,827			
Administrative expense	11,906	7,500			4,406
Fixed charges	3,131	3,131			
Books	5,375	5,375			
	62,434,425	57,114,203	—	1,274,619	4,045,603

Transfers

Transfers from general fund of net restricted tax revenues	$ 8,905,116	$ 6,543,222	$	$2,361,894	$
Transfers to general fund	(495,000)		(495,000)		
Net transfers among plant funds		1,438,829	(3,050,000)	(1,137,932)	2,749,103
Transfers to bond interest and redemption funds	(3,500)				(3,500)
Other transfers—net	552,945		(6,477)	559,422	
	8,959,561	7,982,051	(3,551,477)	1,783,384	2,745,603
Net increase (decrease)	1,680,674	2,359,728	(1,494,172)	815,118	
Funds balances July 1, 1965	2,054,235		2,054,235		
Independent audit adjustments not recorded by District	85,704	(111,168)	(4,019)	200,891	
Funds balances June 30, 1974	$ 3,820,613	$ 2,248,560	$ 556,044	$1,016,009	—

The accompanying notes are an integral part of these statements and schedules.

SCHEDULE III

Peralta Community College District
Statement of Capital Expenditures by School (Note 4)
for the Eight Fiscal Years Ended June 30, 1973

(Unaudited)

	Total	*Sites*	*Site Improvements*	*Buildings*
Merritt College	$15,371,368	$ 40,486	$ 3,063,035	$12,267,847
Laney College	27,211,284	2,837,174	2,426,447	21,947,663
College of Alameda	12,118,125	3,313,764	1,788,275	7,016,086
North Peralta College	27,335			27,335
Feather River College	245,283		1,470	243,813
Berkeley–Albany Site Selection	43,023	18,489	8,605	15,929
Oakland Airport	11,362	271	2,112	8,979
Warehouse Relocation	12,378			12,378
Unalloted differences (Note 4)	2,529,728	(2,511,030)	3,299,156	1,741,602
(Note 5)	$57,569,886	$3,699,154	$10,589,100	$43,281,632

The accompanying notes are an integral part of these statements and schedules.

SCHEDULE IV

Peralta Community College District
Statement of General Purpose Expenditures
per A.D.A. by School (Notes 6 and 7)
for the Fiscal Years Ended June 30, 1971, 1972, 1973 and 1974

(Unaudited)

School	1971 Total Expenditures	Per A.D.A.	1972 Total Expenditures	Per A.D.A.	1973 Total Expenditures	Per A.D.A.	1974 Total Expenditures	Per A.D.A.
College of Alameda	$2,982,826	833.0	$3,320,762	894.4	$2,869,408	821.9	$3,096,317	726.2
North Peralta College			$1,473,826	1,081.3	$1,319,135	967.8	$1,318,045	1,177.9
Laney College	$6,604,974	883.1	$7,789,580	863.4	$6,810,048	798.8	$7,045,568	830.5
Merritt College	$5,940,510	1,104.6	$5,952,418	1,135.1	$4,732,868	836.5	$5,061,672	809.1
Feather River College	$ 584,223	1,418.0	$1,239,046	2,434.3	$ 806,740	1,527.9	$ 834,362	1,352.3

The accompanying notes are an integral part of these statements and schedules.

99

SCHEDULE V

Peralta Community College District
Statement of General Purpose Revenue,
Expenditures and Deficit for Feather River College
for the Six Fiscal Years Ended June 30, 1974

(Unaudited)

Total net revenues (Note 8)	$4,807,793
Total expenditures (Note 8)	6,699,308
Deficit	$1,891,515

The accompanying notes are an integral part of these statements and schedules.

SCHEDULE VI

Peralta Community College District
Statement of Assumptions Underlying 1965 Bond Requirements

(Unaudited)

Average cost per student for junior college construction	$3,000	
Anticipated full-time students	12,000	
Therefore estimated construction costs were computed as follows:		
12,000 × $3,000 =		$36,000,000
Add estimated site acquisition costs:		11,000,000
Total Bond Requirements		$47,000,000
A.D.A. for North Peralta College 1972 and 1973–	1,363 students	
1,363 × $3,000 per student =	$4,089,000	

The accompanying notes are an integral part of these statements and schedules.

SCHEDULE VII

Peralta Community College District
Statement of Federal and State Grant Revenue
for the Nine Fiscal Years Ended June 30, 1974

(Unaudited)

Capital Fund

State Junior College Construction Act of 1965 (Stern Act)	$2,269,939
Higher Education Facilities Act of 1963	762,574
Vocational Education Act	426,608
Department of Housing and Urban Development— Open Space Grant	247,097
Department of Health, Education and Welfare	237,426
Higher Education Act of 1965	91,166
National Defense Education Act	41,753
Allied Health Professions	26,506
Other	9,352
Adjustment to Fund Balance by independent auditors	30,694
	4,143,115
Entitlement under Junior College Construction Act of 1965	353,600

Special Reserve Fund No. 1

Forest Reserve	145,000
	$4,641,715

The accompanying notes are an integral part of these statements and schedules.

Peralta Community College District
Notes to Statements and Schedules

1. Sources of Financial Information:

Schedule Title	*Period*	*Source of Data*
I. Plant Funds Balance Sheet	June 30, 1974	California Community Colleges Annual Financial and Budget Report (CCAF-301)
II. Statements of Changes in Plant Funds Balances	For the nine fiscal years ended June 30, 1974	Annual Audited Financial Statements and California Community Colleges Annual Financial and Budget Report (CCAF-301)

Peralta Community College District
Notes to Statements and Schedules
(Continued)

III. Statement of Capital Expenditures by School

For the eight fiscal years ended June 30, 1973

Detail of Capital Outlay—All Funds

IV. Statement of General Purpose Expenditures per A.D.A. by School

For each of the fiscal years ended June 30, 1971, 1972, 1973 and 1974

Budget Status Report Summary, and, except for 1974 A.D.A., Annual A.D.A. Actual. For 1974 A.D.A. First Period A.D.A. Actual

V. Statement of General Purpose Revenue and Expenditures For Feather River College

For the six fiscal years ended June 30, 1974

"Analysis of Revenue and Expenditures for the Feather River College for years 1968–1969 Through Estimates for 1973–1974" prepared by Alanson T. Powell

VI. Statement of Assumptions Underlying Computation of 1965 Bond Requirements

N/A

Pamphlet Entitled "Some Questions Which May be Raised in Regard To The Bond Proposal For the Peralta Colleges and Suggestions As To How They Can Be Answered"

VII. Statement of Federal and State Grant Revenue

For the nine fiscal years ended June 30, 1974

Annual Audited Financial Statements, County Cash Statements, Cash Receipt Journal and County of Alameda Miscellaneous Receipt copies

2. District Personnel Interviewed:

In addition to the various accounting and financial records mentioned in Note 1, information was obtained and/or discussions were held concerning the data presented herein with the following District personnel:

Name	Title
Thomas W. Fryer, Jr.	Chancellor
Dr. Clement A. Long	Vice Chancellor, Administrative & Business Services
Ray Rubard	Internal Auditor
Alanson T. Powell	Director, Fiscal Services
Robert F. Batchelder	Controller
Ed Dankworth	Director, Facilities Planning

3. Plant Funds Balances:

The plant funds group consists of unexpended funds to be used for the acquisition of properties and equipment. Acquisitions of physical properties and equipment financed from the plant funds group are not capitalized and are recorded as plant funds expenditures.

The District has not maintained historical cost records with respect to its investment in institutional plant. Accordingly, the District has not included such assets in its plant funds financial statements. This school district practice is at variance with generally accepted accounting principles and results in the understatement of assets.

It is generally accepted accounting principle for colleges and universities not to record depreciation of institutional plant and equipment as a charge against current operations. Accordingly, no provision for such depreciation has been made.

The purpose of each fund is as follows:

Capital Fund—All funds received for major building programs, including proceeds from general obligation bond issues and override taxes, are recorded in this fund. The Board of Trustees has reserved $500,000 for acquisition of a site for relocation of North Peralta College.

Special Reserve No. 1—The Education Code provides that a portion of nonresident tuition be recorded in this fund and used only for capital outlay purposes. Amounts in the fund from other sources may be used for general purposes.

Special Reserve No. 2—Reserved by the Board of Trustees for capital outlay relating to community services. Unexpended community services override taxes are transferred to this fund; the Education Code provides that such funds may be expended only for community services purposes.

Student Center Construction Fund—The Student Center Construction Funds for Alameda, Laney and Merritt were established with District contributions and College Housing Loans. All three Student Center buildings were completed in 1970–71 and the funds were closed.

4. During the eight fiscal years ended June 30, 1973, the District maintained on an individual school basis a subsidiary ledger for capital expenditures in connection with sites, improvement of sites, and buildings. In the opinion of District Management, however, the internal accounting control surrounding the maintenance of this record was inadequate, and as a result the ledger

Peralta Community College District
Notes to Statements and Schedules
(Continued)

totals do not agree with total capital expenditures as reflected on the annual financial statements.   This record was not maintained during the fiscal year ending June 30, 1974.

5. Campus Construction Costs:

	Total	Sites	Site Improvements	Buildings
Total campus construction expenditures for the eight fiscal years ended June 30, 1973:				
From plant funds	$57,167,035	$3,608,386	$10,573,900	$42,984,749
From general fund	402,851	90,768	15,200	296,883
	$57,569,886	$3,699,154	$10,589,100	$43,281,632

6. General Purpose Expenditures:

The general purpose expenditures at the school level are comprised of the following cost classifications:

Presidents' and deans' salaries
Coordinators' and department chairmen's salaries
Instructors' salaries
Other certificated salaries of instruction
Instructional aides' salaries
Other classified salaries of instruction
Other books
Other expenses of instruction
Other expenses of health services
Other expenses of pupil transportation
Classified salaries for operation of plant
Other expenses for operation of plant
Replacement of equipment
Other expenses of maintenance of plant
Other fixed charges
Meals for needy pupils
Classified salaries of community services
Other expenses of community services
Economic Opportunity agency expenses
Buildings
Equipment

7. Average Daily Attendance:

School	1971	1972	1973	1974
College of Alameda	3,581	3,713	3,491	4,264
North Peralta College	–	1,363	1,363	1,119
Laney College	7,479	9,022	8,525	8,484
Merritt College	5,378	5,244	5,658	6,256
Feather River College	412	509	528	617

8. Feather River College—General Purpose Revenue and Expenditures:

Total net revenues include state apportionment, deduction from Peralta equalization, local taxes, Forest Reserve Funds, tuition transfers, non-resident fees, and health fees.

Total expenditures include pro rata cost of district administration, all instruction, health, transportation, operation, maintenance, food services, community services, capital outlay, all leasing payments for building occupancy, pro rata share of warehousing costs, and tuition paid.

Total expenditures do not include the following purchases:

Item Purchased	Cost
Alarm and security system installation	$37,000
Lease-purchase of a pickup and station wagon	3,362
36-passenger school bus	15,550
Loader-snow removal truck	16,101
	$72,013

Revenues and expenditures for 1973–74 are estimates.

The Outcome

On September 10, 1974, a lawsuit was filed against the Board of Trustees of the Peralta Community College District. The petitioners in this legal action were the Associated Students of North Peralta College; Congressman Ronald Dellums; Warren Widener, Mayor of Berkeley; Ying Lee Kelley and Loni Hancock, Berkeley City Council members; and Maudelle Shirck as a representative of voters and taxpayers of the Peralta Community College District.

This action sought an order requiring the Board of Trustees to comply with their fiduciary and contractual duty to establish and maintain a full scale degree-granting college in the northern part of the district; to provide the students and residents of the North Peralta District an educational opportunity equal to that afforded students and residents in other areas of the district; and to repay to the voters and taxpayers of the district more than $10,000,000, which represented the revenues from construction bonds approved by the voters in the 1965 bond proposal that allegedly had been unlawfully diverted by the trustees from the North Peralta Campus.

The SF API volunteer assisted the Legal Aid Society in formulating questions for depositions and interrogatories and in obtaining admissions of financial data in connection with the suit. He also provided expert testimony related to the report during the trial.

In late 1975, the judge decided in favor of the district, using the narrow legal issue of what constitutes the contract between the district and the voters. He ruled that the contract was limited to the language contained in the bond resolution itself, rather than some contrary representations concerning the use of bond proceeds admittedly made by the trustees and a related citizens advisory committee prior to the vote on the bond issue. The decision will be appealed by the Alameda County Legal Aid Society.

In an evaluation letter, the Legal Aid Society wrote:

Of tantamount importance to our client's position and to the realistic prospects of any lawsuits was the question: "Did Peralta have any money left with which it could either build or refurbish a community college in the Berkeley-Albany area?"

The answer to that question dictated whether or not it would be feasible to continue, either on a political or legal level.

[API's volunteer] did a substantial amount of work determining the answer to that question, and was able to give us an answer we could use in spite of the roadblocks he faced. Among the roadblocks . . . Peralta's books were not in the best of shape, and . . . Peralta had used certain procedures that do not comply with generally accepted accounting principles.

The answer . . . was that . . . Peralta had a significant amount of money left, enough to at least refurbish the Grove St. Campus so that Peralta could provide community college services to students living in the Berkeley-Albany area.

Later, after the case was filed, [the API volunteer] assisted in preparing written interrogatories to Peralta concerning their financial condition. Those were of great value to us in that they conclusively showed that Peralta's building funds were not as bankrupt as Peralta had previously claimed.

In short, the help provided by API volunteers was invaluable to the effort . . .

Although the specifics encountered in this case are unlikely to occur frequently elsewhere, it is apparent that electorates everywhere can learn an important lesson from this study and the court's decision. It is incumbent on the voters to insist on full, complete, and specific disclosures in any bond resolution concerning any representations made as to how bond funds may be disbursed.

_____(9)_____

An Open Space Issue

The difficulty in identifying a single "public interest" is highlighted by a case involving open space. On one side stood the conservationists, espousing open space and decrying overcrowding and environmental pollution. They clearly represented a "public interest." The opposition was led by developers and labor unions seeking business expansion and jobs for construction workers—another "public interest." In between was the biggest "public" in the controversy: the electorate who pay property taxes and who were being asked to vote on a bond issue for the acquisition of land for open space without any information on the financial impact of their decision.

The client did not necessarily represent the biggest public, or the most important public, or the "right" public. It simply was "in the public interest" to provide data to help the decision makers—in this case the voters—to become better informed on this complex issue.

A Dispute Arises

The dispute, which arose in late 1974, concerned Corte Madera, a town in Marin County, California, just across the Golden Gate Bridge north of San Francisco. The bond issue was for $1 million to acquire certain parcels of land to preserve as open space that otherwise would be sold for residential and commercial development. The client was the Marin Conservation League, an organization leading the fight for the bond issue. MCL had been active in preserving land for open-space uses, both through acquisition and through assisting government at various levels in planning. Their work had resulted in the provision of beaches, parks, and wild areas for Marin County. Along with the town of Corte Madera, the cities of Larkspur and Mill Valley, and Marin County, the League had produced the Northridge Open Space Plan. This involved the acquisition of 1,300 acres in the vicinity of an especially beautifully scenic area, Mt. Tamalpais. Part of the proceeds of the $1 million bond

107

issue would go toward the purchase of that part of Northridge that lay within the boundaries of Corte Madera.

In addition to the traditional environmental arguments in favor of the open space proposed, MCL held that the cost of providing services to the residents of the new development would exceed the tax revenues it generated, and they hoped that an independent demonstration of that premise would assure victory at the ballot. They also wanted to know the estimated effect on the property tax rates if the land was acquired for open space by means of the proposed bond issue. Marin County voters had frequently supported environmental causes at the polls and could be expected to do so again, particularly if the economics were right.

The API executive committee, which considered the case at its regular meeting on November 27, was disposed to undertake the assignment, but the case neatly illustrated certain recurring problems. First was the time element. API already had a heavy work schedule. The deadline MCL at first proposed was December 31, which allowed barely five weeks to complete the fieldwork and report. A one-month extension was possible, but even this created difficulties because it meant that the demands of the busy tax season would be competing for the attention of the volunteers. To complicate matters, API was just then preparing for a change in executive directors, which was to be effective January 1, 1975, and probably meant at least some disruption in operations. Second, those assigned to the case would have to master quickly the mass of complex material the league had supplied to API. In the end, more than twenty documents—audits, budgets, reports—figured in the study.

Nevertheless, the committee agreed to accept the case, if the staff could establish the detailed assumptions that would underlie the study and get the league's agreement to them. These assumptions were worked out between the API participants in the case—one staff member, two professional volunteers, and one student volunteer—and various officials of Corte Madera. Thus, the meetings also served to establish contacts with the town manager, treasurer, city planner, and department heads, and to explore problems that might arise during the work.

On January 9, 1975, API wrote to MCL to set out the terms of the engagement:

We will estimate the effect on the property tax rate in Corte Madera resulting from the acquisition of designated parcels of land for open space, and park and recreational land through a bond issue, and compare such effect with estimates, also prepared by us, of the net effect to the property tax rate, if any, if the land is developed in accordance with current zoning requirements.

In this connection, the following represents a list of general assumptions, the basis upon which our analysis will proceed. With respect to the Open Space Alternative, our understanding is as follows:

1) All land will be purchased;
2) The subject land, if purchased, will be left as is;
3) There will be some type of annual maintenance and insurance cost;
4) The proposed bond issue will not cover the entire cost of land;
5) Details of assumed matching-fund arrangements will be provided to us;
6) The bond issue will be $1,000,000 face value, with a twenty-five year maturity at an interest rate of 7 percent, with a principal to be repaid serially over the life of the bonds.

With respect to the Residential-Development alternative our understanding is as follows:

1) The development will be totally residential (i.e. no shopping centers, etc.);
2) The following information, or access to it, will be provided by officials of the City of Corte Madera:
    a) Relevant cost data for increased needs, if any, regarding social services (i.e. police and fire protection, education, sanitation, city equipment and staff, etc.);
    b) Clear and distinct allocation of responsibility and financial burden between the City, the Developer . . . etc.;
    c) Estimated assessed valuations throughout the period of development.
3) All of the subject land will be developed at the lowest density level as presently permitted by zoning laws.

The letter closed with a careful spelling out of the conditions under which API would work. It took note of the time problems, and the possibility that some new assumptions might be added. In language that has become familiar, it reminded the client that the work would be conducted in an "objective, independent, nonadvocative manner," and that API could not vouch for the reliability of the data used, or the extent to which they had been assembled in accordance with "generally accepted accounting principles." In other words, API was making its study relying on data supplied by the parties involved in the dispute and made no independent attempt to establish their validity. As usual, API reserved the right to publish the report itself, and to approve any excerpting or condensation made by the client.

As the field work unfolded and more meetings were held, some assumptions were clarified and others added. These were listed in a letter to the league on January 17:

With respect to the Residential Development alternative, our understanding is as follows:

I. *Projected Number of Units Under Residential Development—937*
  A. Properties for which development plans have already been formulated—
     837, as follows:

Development Plan	*Units*
Madera Del Presidio	325
Deffebach's properties	42
Ring Mountain	94
Kock properties	189
Evergreen	34
La Cresta	153
Total	837

  B. All other properties based on current zoning requirements—*100,* as
     follows:

Parcel No.	*°Acreage To Be Developed (Rounded)*	*Units Per Acre Per Zoning*	*Units (Rounded)*
25-241-47			
25-241-46			
25-251-01			
25-251-02	12	2	24
25-251-04			
25-181-38			
25-231-07	3	6	17
25-222-01	5	2	11
38-240-01	6	6	39
38-240-02			
26-053-07	.2	11	3
26-053-13	.5	11	6
			100

°Based upon the assumption that minimum lot sizes exclude road
areas which are estimated to equal approximately 25% of gross
acreage.

II. *Rate of Residential Development*
  A. In connection with the 837 units for which plans have already been
     formulated, development will occur proratably over the eight years
     ending June 30, 1983, or 105 units per year.
  B. In connection with all other properties, development will occur at the
     rate of 2 percent per year or two units per year. At the end of
     twenty-five years, fifty units will be completed and fifty units will be
     completed subsequent to June 30, 2000.

III. *Average Population Per Housing Unit—3.*
IV. *Average Fair Market Value of Housing Unit Upon Completion—$75,000.*
V. *All Valuations Will Be Expressed in 1974–75 Dollars.*

With respect to the Open Space alternative our understanding is as follows:

I. Annual maintenance cost to the Town of Corte Madera for open space acquisitions is estimated to be $75.00 per acre.
II. Matching funds, if any, provided by the Marin County Open Space District will come from existing budget allocations.
III. The assessed valuation for the Town of Corte Madera used in determining the tax rate necessary to service the bond debt and interest is $42,004,745 in 1975–76. This amount was computed by officials of the Town of Corte Madera and takes into consideration a 5 percent normal assessed valuation increase due to improvements, tax delinquencies, and the removal of open space properties from the tax rolls.

The letter also requested an extension of the deadline, which was granted.

The report was issued on February 16, ten days after a draft was circulated to the client and town treasurer for their comments. It included a "Summary of Assumptions and Projections":

Accountants for the Public Interest has projected the effect of the March 1975 open space bond proposal on property tax rates in Corte Madera. Our projection differs from that of the Treasurer of the Town of Corte Madera largely because we used an estimated, average assessed valuation over the life of the bond issue, rather than the current assessed valuation. We do not intend to update or revise this projection for events after January 31, 1975.

We believe that the projections were compiled in all material respects to give effect to the assumptions described below, which were arrived at by interviewing responsible officials. The assumptions are about future events, based on present circumstances and available information. We do not express an opinion on the reasonableness or comprehensiveness of those assumptions.

Projections are inherently subject to varying degrees of uncertainty and their achievability depends on the timing and probability of a complex series of future events, both internal and external. Accordingly, we do not express an opinion on the achievability of the projections or on the probability that the actual results for any period may or may not approximate the projections. Twenty-five years is a very long period over which to attempt projections. Accordingly, there is an especially high degree of uncertainty attached to such projections.

Assumptions

By interviews with responsible officials, we obtained assumptions regarding changes to be expected over the twenty-five year period of our forecast which are directly caused by acquisition of the land for open space or development of the land.

A. *Assumptions Applicable to Both Alternatives*
1. Increases in assessed valuation due to improvements in currently developed areas will occur at the rate of 3.5 percent per year, compounded annually, for the twenty-five years ending June 30, 2000. The average cumulative increase over the 1974–75 assessed valuation is 58 percent.
2. All estimates are expressed in [1975] dollars, ignoring the effect of inflation. We believe that inflation would probably reduce the impact of the bond issue on the taxpayer, while not changing the impact of development significantly.
3. Each taxing district will continue to finance its operations with the same proportion of property taxes and other revenues. Each item of expenditure is financed proportionately by the property tax and other general revenues, except as explained in 4 and 5 below.
4. The open space bond issue is treated as entirely financed from the property tax, because the Tax Reform Act of 1973 (California Law SB90) permits a rise in the maximum rate to cover the cost. The town of Corte Madera is currently 8¢ below its maximum rate.
5. Planning and inspection costs are treated as financed by the related fees charged to builders.

B. *Open Space Alternative*
1. All parcels will be purchased by the Town evenly over the first three years after issuance of the bonds.
2. All parcels will remain in their present condition.
3. Annual maintenance cost to the Town is estimated to be $6,600.
4. Additional needed funds, if any, will be provided by the Marin County Open Space District. These funds will not cause a change in the property tax rate for the district.
5. The bond issue will be $1,000,000 face value, with a twenty-five year maturity and an interest rate of 6.5 percent with one principal and two interest payments annually. It will be paid for entirely by the property tax.
6. Net proceeds of the bond issue would be $975,000. Unused proceeds during the first three years will be invested at 6⅝ percent.

C. *Residential Development Alternative*
1. Developers will bear the entire cost of development, which will consist of utilities, roads, land preparation and construction of 937 projected housing units, as follows:
   a. 837 units on properties for which development plans have been filed, at the rate of 105 units per year for the eight years ending June 30, 1983.
   b. 100 units on other properties at the rate of two units per year for the fifty years ending June 30, 2025.
   Thus, there would be an average of 745 completed and occupied units in existence during any one year over the twenty-five year period ending

June 30, 2000. This rate of development may exceed the capacity of water and sewage treatment facilities.

2. Average population per housing unit—three persons, with ages as in the 1970 census for Corte Madera.
3. Average assessed valuations of each housing unit upon completion (net of Homeowner's Exemption, if any)—$12,500.

Projections

The projections relate to Corte Madera residents of the Larkspur Elementary School District. Corte Madera residents in other elementary districts will have slightly higher net tax benefits from development.

If the open space bond measure is passed by the voters of Corte Madera, we estimate that, on a twenty-five year average, a resident's total tax rate would be increased by $.136 per $100 of assessed valuation ($17.00 to a homeowner with a $12,500 taxable valuation). This potential increase is the net effect of payments to bondholders, income from investment of idle bond proceeds, removal of land from the tax rolls, and maintenance of the open land.

If the open space bond measure is not passed, and the properties are developed in accordance with the above assumptions, we estimate that, on a twenty-five year average, a resident's total tax rate would be decreased by $.140 per $100 of assessed valuation ($17.50 to a homeowner with a $12,500 taxable valuation). This assessed valuation has also been adjusted upward for yearly increases due to improvements on currently developed areas. This potential decrease is the net result of additional revenue (resulting from the development) and additional costs for taxing districts. Whether the benefit is used to lower tax rates or to fund unrelated increases in costs, is up to the governing body of each taxing district.

The summary was followed by a detailed description of supporting data, a list of the officials and other expects with whom the API staff had met, and a list of all the documents used in the study.

I. *Our Approach to the Projections*
  A. *Open Space Alternative*
    The sale of a $1,000,000 general obligation bond issue by the Town of Corte Madera (Town) and using the proceeds, together with County open space funds, to purchase the parcels of land designated in the Corte Madera bond issue proposition to be voted on in March 1975, and preserving this land in its present state is the *Open Space Alternative*.
    The effect upon the property taxpayer in the Town resulting from the selection of this alternative is the net effect of the following factors:
    1. *Annual Debt Service*
      The town will necessarily levy a tax to pay the principal and interest on the bonds annually.
      We estimated the debt service cost based upon the bond maturity date, assumed interest rate, and the total number of principal

and interest payments to be made over the life of the bonds. We determined the annual cost to the Town by use of an amortization table. This annual cost was then translated into a rate per $100 of assessed valuation.

2. *Annual Open Space Maintenance Cost*

The Town will incur an additional annual cost to maintain the land in its present state (annual open space maintenance cost).

We estimated the annual open space maintenance cost, based upon the actual experience of similar maintenance activities within the County of Marin. This annual cost was then translated into a rate per $100 of assessed valuation.

3. *Additional Tax Burden on Remaining Property Owners*

The property owners in the Town will receive an additional tax burden because the subject land will be removed from the tax rolls.

We selected tax code areas 2.000, 2.004 and 2.018, which account for more than 95 percent of the total Corte Madera tax base. Based upon the 1974–75 budgeted revenues, we determined, for each taxing district, the increase in tax rate necessary to raise the same amount of local tax revenue, if the total tax base were reduced by the assessed valuation of the proposed open space land.

B. *Residential Development Alternative*

Allowing the designated parcels of land to remain privately owned with the expectation that the land will be developed in accordance with current plans and zoning requirements is the *Residential Development Alternative.*

The effect upon the property taxpayer in the Town resulting from the selection of this alternative is the net effect of the following factors:

1. *Additional Property Tax Revenue*

The taxes received by the Town and other taxing districts whose local tax revenue comes from the Town property owners will be increased because improvements on the designated parcels of land will increase the tax base.

Based upon an assumed fair market value of a completed housing unit on the designated parcels of land we estimated the tax revenues generated to each of the respective taxing districts. This additional tax revenue was then translated into a rate per $100 of assessed valuation.

2. *Additional Governmental Services Costs*

Certain costs of the respective taxing districts will increase because of their obligation to provide specific community services to the area to be developed. We assumed that the current portion of costs provided by property taxes in each taxing district would continue to apply.

We interviewed officials of the most significant taxing districts regarding the potential cost increase to the districts directly attributable to the projected increase in housing units and population. The results of each interview were summarized in a letter to the official interviewed. Based upon the interviews and current financial data for the district, this cost was converted into a rate per $100 of assessed valuation.

The housing unit and population projections for the respective taxing districts were estimated in the following manner:

1. *Housing Units on Land Parcels for Which Specific Development Plans Have Already Been Formulated*

   We determined the number of these units by reliance upon development plans, the Town's General Housing Plan and interviews with appropriate Town officials.

2. *Other Housing Units*

   We computed the net acreage to be developed taking into consideration the size of each of the designated parcels and land portions which will be used for roads. Our computation was discussed and confirmed with appropriate Town officials.

3. *Population*

   Population was projected by applying a residents-per-unit estimate to the estimated number of housing units.

II. *Description of Projections*

  A. *Applicable to Both Alternatives*

    Average assessed valuation for one year over twenty-five years ending June 30, 2000, based upon a 3.5 percent annual rate of increase, compounded annually, due to improvements, is as follows:

	Assessed Valuation		
Taxing District	*Excluding Subject Development*	*Assumed Development*	*Total*
County of Marin	$1,533,651,000	$9,008,640	$1,542,659,640
Town of Corte Madera	64,846,000	9,008,640	73,854,640
Larkspur School District	97,752,000	3,250,521	101,002,521
Mill Valley School District	192,524,000	2,932,017	195,456,017
Tamalpais Union High School District	819,311,000	9,008,640	828,319,640
Marin Community College	1,527,253,000	9,008,640	1,536,261,640

  B. *Open Space Alternative*

    1. *Annual Debt Service*

      a. The average annual cost for service of the bonded indebtedness over twenty-five years is $81,981.

      b. Based on a twenty-five year average assessed valuation of

$64,846,000, the Corte Madera tax levy necessary to service the debt would be $.126 per $100 of assessed valuation.

2. *Annual Open Space Maintenance Cost*

Based on an assumed annual maintenance cost to be borne by property tax payers of $2,792 and an average assessed valuation of $64,846,000, the tax levy necessary to maintain the open space parcels in their present condition would be $.004 per $100 of assessed valuation.

3. *Additional Tax Burden on Remaining Property Owners*

The additional tax levy necessary to compensate for a reduction in the tax base caused by removal of open space properties ($303,860 total assessed valuation) from tax rolls is $.012 per $100 of assessed valuation on remaining property in Corte Madera.

C. *Residential Development Alternative*

1. In connection with taxable property located within the Larkspur School District, the additional tax revenue resulting from development totals approximately $.325 per $100 of assessed valuation, as follows:

Taxing District	*Rate per $100 of Assessed Valuation*
County of Marin	$ .014
Town of Corte Madera	.158
Flood Control Zone #9	.001
Mosquito Abatement	.001
Sanitary District #2–General	.044
Marin General Hospital	.001
Sanitary District #2–Bonds	.013
Larkspur School–General	.061
Tamalpais Union High–General	.020
Marin Community College	.006
County School Service Fund	.001
Larkspur School District	.004
Tamalpais Union High School Bonds	.001
	$ .325

The rate is somewhat smaller for taxable property located within the Mill Valley School District.

2. Based upon the current status of educational facilities for the following school districts, the projected attendance increases can be absorbed by the respected districts with no required expansion of existing facilities:

– Larkspur School District (Elementary)
– Reed Union School District (Elementary)

— Mill Valley School District (Elementary)
— Tamalpais Union High School District
— Marin Community College District

Projected increases in cost of education were computed as follows:

School District	Projected Attendance Increase	Cost of Education Per Average Daily Attendant Financed by Local Property Taxes	Projected Increase In Cost of Education borne by Property Owners
Larkspur	130	$ 642	$ 83,460
Mill Valley	220	664	146,080
Tamalpais	192	1,405	269,760
Marin Community College	74	656	48,544

School District	Projected Increase in Cost of Education Borne by Property Owners	Assessed Valuation	Projected Increase in Tax Rate
Larkspur	$ 83,460	$ 101,003,000	$ .083
Mill Valley	146,080	195,456,000	.074
Tamalpais	269,760	828,320,000	.033
Marin Community College	48,544	1,536,262,000	.003

3. We estimated that the annual increase in property tax rates for the Town of Corte Madera (including Sanitary District #2) is $.066/ $100 of assessed valuation, computed as follows:

Description	Amount	Explanation
Fire Department	$ 6,120	Hydrants, alarm and drill pay and supplies cost
Police Department	50,950	Salaries plus fringe benefits for 3 additional patrolmen, 1 additional patrol car, uniforms, supplies.

Description	*Amount*	*Explanation*
Public Works	26,212	Street light maintenance, sewer maintenance, sewage processing, additional vehicle maintenance
Average Cost over 25 Years for Capital Improvements	32,195	Street resurfacing, street widening, upgrading and clearance of storm facilities, increase in sewage capacity
Average Yearly Cost over 25 years	$115,477	
Percentage of Town Costs Financed by Local Property Taxes	42.3%	
Average Yearly Cost Over 25 Years Financed by Local Property Taxes	$48,847	
25-Year Average Assessed Valuation Including Development of Open Lands	$73,855,000	
Estimated Increase in Tax Rate	$.066/$100 of assessed valuation	

D. *API projections*

Town of Corte Madera
Estimated Average Annual Tax Increase for
Open Space Alternative

Estimated Cost (Revenue)	*Rate per $100 Assessed Valuation*	*Taxed Assessed Valuation of Property*[1]				
		$7,500	*$10,000*	*$12,500*	*$15,000*	*$17,500*
Debt Service	$ .126					
Interest on Idle Proceeds	(.006)					
Removal of Property From Rolls	.012					
Annual Maintenance of Open Space	.004					
Net Increase Based on 25-Year Average Assessed Valuation	$ .136	$10.20	$ 13.60	$ 17.00	$ 20.40	$ 23.80

Town of Corte Madera
Estimated Average Annual Tax Decrease for
Residential Development Alternative

Estimated Cost (Revenue)	Rate Per $100 Assessed Valuation	Taxed Assessed Valuation of Property[1]				
		$7,500	$10,000	$12,500	$15,000	$17,500
Revenue						
Increase	$ (.325)					
Cost Increase						
Town of Corte Madera[2]	.066					
Larkspur Schools	.083					
Tamalpais Schools	.033					
Marin Community College	.003					
Net Decrease Based on 25-Year Average Assessed Valuation	$ (.140)	$(10.50)	$(14.00)	$(17.50)	$(21.00)	$(24.50)

1. Homeowner's Exemption not considered.
2. Including Sanitary District #2.

Reports

1974–1975 Final Budget and Auditor-Controller's Financial Report for the Year Ended June 30, 1974, County of Marin, California

Distribution of 1974–1975 Property Tax Dollars compiled by Michael Mitchell, Auditor-Controller, County of Marin

Environmental Impact Report, Madera Del Presidio Planned Unit Development, Sedway/Cooke

The Costs of Sprawl, Executive Summary, based upon a report, *The Cost of Sprawl: Detailed Cost Analysis* prepared by Real Estate Research Corporation

Open Space vs. Development, Final Report to the City of Palo Alto, Foothills Environmental Design Study, Livingston and Blayney, City and Regional Planners.

Reed Union School District 1974–75 Budget

Study and Evaluation of the Fire Defense Program for the Town of Corte Madera, Ingram & Associates, Consulting Engineers

Town of Corte Madera, 1974–75 Budget and Report for 1973–74

Master Drainage Plan for the Bel Aire Flood Control Zone prepared by the
    Marin County Department of Public Works, Donald R. Frost, Director
Title 18, Zoning
Marin County Statistical Abstract, Marin County Planning Dept.
Town of Corte Madera General Plan
Audited Financial Statements for the Year Ended June 30, 1974 regarding
    the following taxing districts:
    — Town of Corte Madera
    — Larkspur School District
    — Reed School District
    — Mill Valley School District
    — Tamalpais Union High School District
"Listing of Proposed Open Space Properties Located Outside of Corte Madera"
    prepared by Marin Conservation League
"Open Space Data Sheet" prepared by Marin Conservation League
Resolution No. 1618—(A Resolution of the Town of Corte Madera Seeking
    Authorization from the Voters to Incur Bonded Indebtedness for Acquisi-
    tion of Real Property for Open Space and Recreational Purposes in the
    Amount of $1,000,000.)
Corte Madera Assessment Roll for 1974–75

The Outcome

Although the bond issue was favored by 55 percent of the voters, it failed
to carry because it required a two-thirds majority. Both its proponents
and its opponents conceded that the report played a decisive role in the
voters' decisions.

There were several special factors in this case:

— API had to depend upon estimates made by informed city officials
— Incremental costs (those costs necessary to expand an activity from
    one level to another) had to be carefully considered, along with a
    segregation of fixed and variable costs.
— Ephemeral community standards played a significant role in the
    results. For example, standards for police and fire services per
    1,000 residents that were acceptable in 1975 might very well be
    outmoded by 1990, say; yet they had to be factored into the study.

Additionally, decisions had to be made concerning the shift in demands for service occasioned by the shift in population from a stable
number of primarily middle-aged people to a growing and younger group
with their accompanying demands on the school system. The study also
called for an estimate of how a change in the location of housing would
affect transportation needs.

Probably the most controversial assumption was to ignore inflation. This weakness was recognized by SF API; but the cure, a sensitivity analysis using various rates of assumed inflation, was believed to be impractical because of the deadline pressure. Furthermore, this complication in an already complex report could have confused the voters.

Three letters of evaluation were received on this case. The finance director of Corte Madera wrote:

I compliment you on the thoroughness of your study with realization that practically all the data you had to work with from necessity had to be forecast[s]. . . . I concur with the findings based on the fact that the projections you have considered are only information of the events that happened on or before January 31, 1975. Again, let me assure you I will support, in every manner, your findings and congratulate you on a job well done.

The client, understandably, was less than fully pleased:

In accordance with our agreement, we provide the following evaluation of the work you did at the request of the Marin Conservation League.

1. The work was performed on schedule, given the need for an extension because of circumstances mainly beyond the control of API.

2. According to our oral understanding, a letter from API to MCL was to have been provided at the beginning of the project stating some of the general assumptions upon which your analysis was to proceed. We did not receive such a letter until January 9, 1975, about two weeks after the project began. One vital assumption, that the property taxpayer would bear only 42.3 percent of additional town costs for services and improvements necessitated under the residential alternative, was not provided MCL prior to receipt of the draft report of February 10, 1975. We objected to this assumption because the largest part of the revenue for the Town of Corte Madera, other than the property tax, is derived from sales tax revenue, the latter chiefly generated by the large area-wide Corte Madera Shopping Center and the auto agencies. Additional residential units will not produce appreciable amounts of "other" revenue. In fact, the Town estimates that sales tax revenue is declining. This means that the bulk of additional costs generated by development will be borne by the property taxpayers. This point was discussed with [API staff] the day after MCL received the draft report.

3. Although API's final report stated that the proposed residential development may exceed the capacity of water and sewage treatment facilities, no cost estimate was included. A crucial understatement of Town costs attributable to development is due to API's assumption that no additional firemen will be needed even though development will increase the present number of dwelling units by about 25 percent. Both of these are examples of the report's understating the impact of residential development on costs borne by property taxpayers.

4. When MCL requested the study, we were not aware of the difficulty of carrying out the request under the conditions of a severe time restraint and problems in securing valid data. From the superior vantage point of hindsight, we believe that while API can contribute to a study of this nature, it was not fair to ask it to assume major responsibility for what is, in essence, a planning function.

I would add that [the API staff and volunteers] worked hard and productively, but did not have the data and support needed.

The final letter was received from Corte Madera's municipal-financing consultants, Hornblower and Weeks-Hemphill, Noyes Incorporated. Their compliments are especially noteworthy, since the defeat of the proposal meant that they lost the opportunity for a substantial commission from the sale of the bonds.

As financial advisors to the Town of Corte Madera we were quite interested in the report your corporation prepared which analyzed the impact on property taxes if the town acquired certain properties for preservation as open space. After reviewing the report I felt that it was both accurate and objective, and it fairly presented the impact on property owners and public agencies if the project were undertaken.

I realize how difficult it is to undertake a project of this type and I think you did a commendable job.

This case illustrates the independent role that an API plays vis-à-vis its clients. It also demonstrates the dangers posed by short and crucial deadlines. Finally, since it showed API how difficult it is to account for every contingency in an unknown future, it offers a new perspective to those who ordinarily find themselves in the more comfortable position of analyzing and criticizing the projections prepared by others.

___(**10**)___

Public Power

Public power plants and services experienced rapid growth in the early part of the twentieth century. By 1920, over 3,000 cities in the United States were in the power business. That number has dwindled to about 2,000 today through consolidation or sales to neighboring private companies. However, such large cities as Los Angeles, Memphis, Seattle, Cleveland, and San Antonio still run on public power, and all electric distribution facilities in Nebraska are consumer-owned.

In 1898, the citizens of the city and county of San Francisco ratified section 119 of the city charter which stated that "it is the declared purpose and intention of the people of the city and county that public utilities shall be gradually acquired and ultimately owned by the city and county."[1] The city then moved to acquire its own water and power system. Congress ultimately responded with the Raker Act in 1913 granting to San Francisco the right to use federal lands to create a water and power source in the Hetch Hetchy Valley (in Stanislaus National Forest and Yosemite National Park), as well as easements for commercial distribution from the sources. Section 9 of the act obligated the city and county to "develop and use hydroelectric power for the use of its people."

San Francisco built a powerhouse in 1925 and constructed a transmission line about 100 miles long from it to a power substation owned by a private utility, Pacific Gas and Electric Company (PG&E), in Newark, California, about 40 miles from San Francisco. It was then announced that construction funds were exhausted, and the Board of Supervisors approved the sale of Hetch Hetchy power to PG&E at Newark. PG&E continued the transmission lines to San Francisco and resold the power to San Francisco consumers.

Several proposed bond issues to create a municipal electrical distribution system in San Francisco were defeated at the polls in the next fifteen years, with the help of heavy, and understandable, opposition from PG&E.

1. Section 119 was amended in 1932 by the insertion of the words "when public interest and necessity demand" at this point.

In 1940, the Supreme Court in *United States vs the City and County of San Francisco* held that the arrangement with PG&E violated section 6 of the Raker Act, which forbids San Francisco to sell power to a private corporation for resale. The court reaffirmed the intent of the act to supply citizens of San Francisco with their own power at the lowest possible rates.

The city nonetheless subsequently entered into contracts under which over 50 percent of Hetch Hetchy power was sold in 1971 to the Turlock and Modesto Irrigation Districts (which resold it to their customers at an annual profit of many millions). About one quarter was sold to out-of-town industrial customers. The balance was carried over PG&E lines for San Francisco municipal services, at an annual cost to the city of $2 million.

At a time of sharply rising municipal costs and property tax rates and of shrinking center city population, many San Franciscans once again saw public power as a way to bend fiscal means to community ends. Sixty years of legal complications led them to seek legal counsel from the San Francisco Neighborhood Legal Assistance Foundation (SFNLAF) whose attorneys decided that success lay through the political process. The first step was to convince the City and County Board of Supervisors to spend $175,000 to $250,000 for an engineering feasibility study to determine the financial results of a municipal acquisition of the PG&E electrical distribution system. Furthermore, a convincing case for economic advantage was essential to motivate politicians to oppose such a large and powerful corporation. Accordingly, in mid-1972 SFNLAF turned to San Francisco Accountants for the Public Interest, only six weeks after API's doors were officially opened. After discussions with the client had clarified the questions to be answered, the executive committee accepted the assignment on June 20, 1972, promising a report by the end of the year.

The policy problems and pragmatic concerns in this case rivalled the obvious technical problems, and were intertwined with them. At this early stage, API was still developing ideas on how it would operate and on the format for the agreement. The request letter was brief, and the engagement letter did not specify API's independent status or claim the right to release the report if the findings contradicted the client's admittedly preconceived notions. The size and complexity of the case also caused concern. There was no way of estimating the time needed (it turned out to be over 500 hours), which complicated the recruitment and assignment of volunteers. These concerns were resolved to the satisfaction of the executive committee.

API was well aware of the private utility industry's vigorous opposition to anyone associated with an effort to municipalize any of its properties. The influence of PG&E in the local community was obvious. The company and many of its employees had contributed heavily to political candidates and ballot propositions. Moreover, it was then in the throes of a municipalization fight in nearby Berkeley; a loss there and in San Francisco would seriously diminish its business and set, from the company's viewpoint, an unhappy precedent. Its voice was heard in the councils of local foundations, upon which API expected to depend in its early years.

Many in API would have preferred to take on such a formidable adversary when the organization was a bit more established. The moment of truth came earlier than might have been desirable, but the API concept called for assistance to groups in need if a public interest issue was involved. The controversiality of the matter should affect acceptance of the case no more than the client's expectations should affect the independence and objectivity of API's work and its report.

The technical problems centered around access—which posed a paradox. Great masses of data were available from local, state, and federal agencies, and from advocates of both public power and private power who had gathered them to "prove" their opposing views. Almost all of the directly pertinent information was in the hands of PG&E, which was understandably reluctant to make it available.

Certain data appeared in reports filed with the state Public Utilities Commission, including annual revenues received from each service area. The revenues received from San Francisco, about $69.5 million in 1971, soon became one of the central factors in the study. Much of the rhetoric by both sides had attempted to compare average private and public power rates, or to show the "profits" made by public power cities, or their lower property tax rates. Little attention was given to the interdependence of these factors. How real are the "profits" of a public power city if its utility rates are much higher and its property tax rates are much lower than those in a comparable private power city? By assuming no change in the private power rate structure after acquisition, API eliminated a weakness of the previous debates and shifted the focus to more meaningful information.

API also devised a fairly simple system to facilitate comparisons of operating results between public power cities and private power cities in California (see Exhibit D and Schedule D-1). The first step was to determine comparable utility rates for six cities served by private power companies and six nearby cities served by public power. In all cases, the private power company rates were higher. API then computed a simple average of the percentage increase in rates of the public power cities to bring them into line with those of the comparable nearby private power cities. These percentages were then applied to the gross revenues reported by the public power cities and this "additional revenue" was added to the reported cash flow from the existing rate structures before bond amortization. The adjusted "potential cash flow" was divided by "adjusted operating revenues" with results that ranged from 38.4 to 63.7 percent with a simple average of 50.5. For San Francisco this all important figure was 41.5 percent—$28.8 million divided by $69.5 million (See Exhibit A).

In other words, the "cash flow before bond amortization" for San Francisco was lower by 9 percent, or $6.3 million, than the average adjusted results for the six major public power cities in California.

The report also demonstrated (Schedule D-2) that most public power cities had lower property tax rates than did neighboring private power cities.

Unfortunately, almost none of the costs, operating expenses, and profits of the company are reported by service area to the PUC. Therefore, API was forced to rely on national averages for publicly owned utilities, compiled by the Federal Power Commission. Furthermore, these data were available only through 1970, while the case dealt with 1971 revenue. This discrepancy was not crucial, however, because inflation was still relatively low and the averages varied little from year to year.

It was clear from the beginning that API would be unable to establish one of the most important figures relating to economic feasibility of the municipalization—the acquisition cost of the utility company property —which would have to await completion of the engineering feasibility study. On the other hand, API could suggest limits within which the acquisition costs would likely fall, and thus estimate a range of cash flow possibilities to the city. The bases of the limits selected are indicated in the letter to the foundation on page 141 below.

The Report

After intensive review and discussion by the executive committee, API's report was issued on December 20, 1972.

It began by answering specific questions SFNLAF had posed:

1) What are PG&E's revenues from selling power to San Francisco? $60,152,000 in the year 1971.

2) What is PG&E's real rate of return?

The 1971 Financial and Statistical Report of the company lists the following company-wide rates of return (all in percent):

	1971	1970	1969
Average invested capital	6.8	6.5	6.9
Year-end net plant	6.2	5.7	6.2
Average common stock equity	11.3	10.6	11.5
Net income to total revenue	15.4	15.1	16.1

Published Federal Power Commission statistics for all reporting privately owned utilities show the following ratios (1971 data was not yet available from the FPC):

	1970	1969
Net income to total revenues (electric division)	14.7	15.2
Rate of return on common equity	11.8	12.2

3) What is PG&E's assessed value of property in San Francisco?

PG&E's property assessment is determined by the California State Board of Equalization. That agency stated to us that the total PG&E company-wide assessed value in San Francisco for 1972–73 is $81,726,000 . . . confirmed by . . . records of the San Francisco County Tax Collector. The total property tax paid by PG&E to San Francisco for 1972–73 was approximately $10,800,000. We have been unable to determine the amount paid for taxes on the electrical distribution system. According to a representative of PG&E, such taxes totaled $3,139,000 for the tax year 1971–72, the property taxes paid on the Hunters Point and Potrero steam plants amounted to $2,321,000, and the San Francisco business tax paid for 1971 was $676,000.

4) How much tax does PG&E pay to San Francisco and does PG&E pass the tax on to the ratepayers?

See (3) above. The property taxes, as are all other allowable expenses, are paid ultimately by the ratepayer. In addition, the company acts as a collection agent for the city with respect to the 5 percent utility tax.

5) How long would it take to pay off the acquisition costs?

We have been informed by a municipal bond dealer that it would be reasonable to expect to amortize revenue bonds for this purpose over a thirty-five year period.

6) If a projection of net profit for a city-owned utility can be made, can one then estimate what amount can be contributed to the city?

Yes. The assumption we are making for illustrative purposes is that the rates for electricity would be the same as now charged. Then the earnings in excess of bond amortization would be available either to lower property taxes or to expand city services. However, the decision could also be made to lower electric utility rates. The vast majority of public power cities in California use a combination of lower rates and lower property taxes (see Schedule D-1 and D-2).

7) How much power does PG&E supply to San Francisco excluding that power which goes to the municipal utilities and what is the rate per kilowatt hour?

In 1971, PG&E sold 3.29 billion KWHs to San Francisco customers. In addition, the city purchased for its own use from the city owned Hetch Hetchy Water and Power System (for the fiscal year ended June 30, 1972) 478 million KWHs.

The average rates, per KWH in 1971 (in cents) vary between classes of customers and with quantities of consumption.

Class of Customer	San Francisco	Company-wide
Residential	2.44	2.17
Commercial	1.62	1.98
Industrial		.98
All classes	1.83	1.72

San Francisco's 1970 residential rate structure was:

Kilowatt hours	Amount of bill (dollars)	per KWH (cents)
100	3.81	3.81
250	6.20	2.48
500	9.40	1.88
750	12.60	1.68
1000	15.80	1.58

8) Are there any expenses which PG&E must face that a municipal utility does not encounter?

Yes. Certain expenses such as federal income tax and California franchise tax would be eliminated. Bond interest rates are lower for governmental agencies (by approximately 2 percent) than for private utilities because of favorable income tax treatment for the purchasers of government bonds.

Other areas of potential difference based on 1970 data, follow:

Type of Expense	Publicly Owned	Privately Owned
Accounting and collection expense per customer (dollars)	7.98	8.86
Advertising and promotion—percent to revenue	1.01	1.54
Production costs—per KWH (mills)	4.61	4.76
Transmission costs—per KWH (mills)	.15	.23

Certain substantial savings should be possible for San Francisco compared with PG&E system-wide expense because of lower unit costs in a high-density area. System wide, PG&E has an average of 35.4 customers per mile of electric distribution line. In San Francisco, the corresponding figure is 237 per mile. Expenses such as service calls, transportation, meter-reading and others should be lower per unit of power than in a low-density area. The relatively stable growth rate in San Francisco compared to some locations in the PG&E service area experiencing rapid residential, commercial and industrial growth rates would also indicate certain savings, particularly in such items as capital improvements and additions.

Some authorities feel that publicly owned utilities spend less than privately owned utilities for such expenses as:

Salary of chief executive officer
Donations
Outside consulting fees (legal, financial, engineering, sales, etc.)
Publication and distribution of report to stockholders
Industry association dues
Directors' fees
Excursions to construction projects
Company newsletter
Political and related activities
Regulatory commission expense

It should be noted, however, that no comparative statistics appear to be available to substantiate specific differences.

9) Aside from the acquisition costs, what expenses would a municipal utility have that a private utility would not have?

Local taxes (see (3) above) and the franchise fee of approximately $200,000 would be lost to the city if municipalization of the distribution facilities were to occur.

Other areas of potential additional cost would be:

Type of Cost (1970 Data)	Publicly Owned	Privately Owned
Distribution costs—dollars per customer	24.15	22.14
Administrative and general—percent to revenues	6.25	5.87

Seven of the nine largest California public power cities showed lower per customer distribution costs in 1971 than the 1970 national averages (1971 not yet available from FPC) indicated above for either public or private utilities. Five of the same nine cities showed higher ratios of administrative costs to operating revenues than did the 1970 national averages for publicly owned utilities. The other four cities were lower than the 1970 average for privately owned utilities.

City	Distribution costs per customer (dollars)	Administrative expense to operating revenue
Los Angeles	29.80	9.42%
Glendale	16.35	7.86
Riverside	19.42	5.53
Santa Clara	14.81	4.81
Palo Alto	16.38	6.87
Anaheim	18.83	2.43
Alameda	21.63	6.43
Burbank	26.59	5.38
Pasadena	21.18	6.84
Pacific Gas and Electric Company—1970	22.47	4.84

The following exhibits and schedules contain data compiled and analyzed from a variety of published and private documents. The validity or reasonableness of the results projected in Exhibits A and B may be evaluated by comparing them with the data shown on Exhibit D and its supporting schedules.

EXHIBIT A

San Francisco Municipal Electric Facility
Projected Annual Cash Flow before Bond Amortization Assuming
Purchase from PG&E of Needs in Excess of Hetch Hetchy Supply

	From Hetch Hetchy 1.8 *Billion KWH*	*From PG&E* 2.0 *Billion KWH*	*Total*
Operating Revenue @ 1.83¢ per KWH	$32,940,000	$36,600,000	$69,540,000
Operating Expenses:			
Production			
Generated—actual cost— 1971 (equals 1.32 mills per KWH)	2,370,000		2,370,000
Purchased @ 7.45 mills (see Schedule A-1)		14,900,000	14,900,000
Transmission—actual 1971	500,000		500,000
Distribution—288,000 customers @ national average for publicly owned utilities— 1970–$24.15 per customer			6,950,000
Accounting & Collections— @ national average for publicly owned utilities—1970–$7.98 per customer			2,300,000
Sales Promotion & Advertising—@ national average for publicly owned utilities—1970–1.01% of revenue			700,000
Administrative & General— @ national average for publicly-owned utilities—1970–6.25% of revenue			4,350,000
Total Operating Expenses			32,070,000

Operating Income (53.9% of revenues)		37,470,000
Adjustments to reflect changes in city financial data:		
Less—Present cash flow from Hetch Hetchy Water & Power Co.— 1971	(12,120,000)	
Add—Other operating revenue from Hetch Hetchy Water & Power Co.—1971	4,500,000	
Add—Amount presently paid to PG&E for wheeling from Newark	2,000,000	
Less—Local taxes and franchise fee for electric distribution	(4,020,000)	
Add—Income from sales of 200 million KWH to Turlock and Modesto Irrigation Districts— @ 5 mills	1,000,000	
Total Adjustments		(8,640,000)
Total Cash Flow Before Bond Amortization— To Exhibit C		$28,830,000

See Assumptions on Schedule A-1.

SCHEDULE A-1

San Francisco Muncipal Electric Facility
Assumptions for Exhibit A

1) That all revenues are at average rates experienced by PG&E in San Francisco in 1971, including municipal use of 510 million KWH.

2) That 200 million KWH are required for servicing Turlock and Modesto Irrigation Districts (Class 1 only—at cost, per Raker Act) and the balance of the 2 billion capacity of Hetch Hetchy is used for San Francisco customers.

3) That San Francisco purchases its remaining needs of 2 billion KWH from PG&E at same weighted average cost of 7.45 mills per KWH, as was sold to other municipalities in 1971.

4) That no provision for depreciation expense is necessary because it is a non-cash expense. It is assumed that the bond issue would cover acquisition costs plus the next several years costs of capital additions and that subsequent bond issues would be needed to finance further capital additions as necessary.

EXHIBIT B

San Francisco Municipal Electric Facility
Projected Annual Cash Flow before Bond Amortization Assuming Full
Generation Needs from Hetch Hetchy, Hunters Point & Potrero

	From Hetch Hetchy 1.8 Billion KWH	*From H. Pt. & Potrero 2.0 Billion KWH*	*Total*
Operating Revenue @ 1.83¢ per KWH	$32,940,000	$36,600,000	$69,540,000
Operating Expenses:			
Production—generated:			
Actual cost—1971—1.32 mills per KWH	2,370,000		2,370,000
Actual cost—1971—5.23 mills per KWH		10,460,000	10,460,000
Transmission—actual—1971	500,000		500,000
Distribution—see EXHIBIT A			6,950,000
Accounting & Collections— see EXHIBIT A			2,300,000
Sales Promotion & Advertising—see EXHIBIT A			700,000
Administration & General— see EXHIBIT A			4,350,000
Total Operating Expenses			27,630,000

EXHIBIT B (Continued)

	From Hetch Hetchy 1.8 Billion KWH	From H. Pt. & Potrero 2.0 Billion KWH	Total
Operating Income (60.3% of revenues)			41,910,000
Adjustments to reflect changes in city financial data: See EXHIBIT A		(8,640,000)	
Less—Additional property taxes for Hunters Point & Potrero		(2,320,000)	
Add—Sales of excess Hunters Point & Potrero power— 808,000,000 KWH (see assumption 3 below) @ estimated price of 3 mills per KWH		2,420,000	(8,540,000)
Total cash flow before bond amortization—to EXHIBIT C			$33,370,000

Assumptions—
1) Same as EXHIBIT A.
2) Same as EXHIBIT A.
3) Total capacity of Hunters Point & Potrero plants (2,808,000,000 KWH) less the 2 billion KWH needed for San Francisco customers would leave an excess of 808 million available for sale to other users at an average price of 3 mills per KWH.

EXHIBIT C

San Francisco Municipal Electric Facility
Projected Annual Cash Flow after Bond Amortization

Assuming Acquisition of	*Assumed Bond Issue*		
Distribution System Only—	*$100 million*	*$150 million*	*$200 million*
Projected cash flow before bond amortization (EXHIBIT A)	$28,830,000	$28,830,000	$28,830,000
Annual Bond Amortization— 6%–35 years	6,900,000	10,350,000	13,800,000
Projected cash flow after bond amortization	$21,930,000	$18,480,000	$15,030,000

Assuming Acquisition of Distribution System & Potrero & Hunters Point Steam Generating Plants—	*Assumed Bond Issue*		
	$250 million	*$300 million*	*$350 million*
Projected cash flow before bond amortization (EXHIBIT B)	$33,370,000	$33,370,000	$33,370,000
Annual Bond Amortization— 6%–35 years	17,240,000	20,690,000	24,140,000
Projected cash flow after bond amortization	$16,130,000	$12,680,000	$ 9,230,000

EXHIBIT D

San Francisco Municipal Electric Facility
Computation of Potential Cash Flow of Six of the Largest California Public Power Cities Based on Rate Increases to Equal those Rates Paid in Nearby Private Power Cities

	Santa Clara	Glendale	Anaheim	Pasadena	Los Angeles	Riverside
Operating Revenues[1]	$7,690,000	$11,330,000	$14,000,000	$12,870,000	$228,120,000	$11,750,000
% increase to reach rate levels of nearby private power cites (Schedule D-1)	22.8%	39.7%	14.1%	3.8%	29.8%	18.7%
Additional revenue if rate were raised to those of nearby private power cities	$1,750,000	$ 4,500,000	$ 1,970,000	$ 490,000	$ 67,980,000	$ 2,200,000
Cash flow from existing rate structures before bond amortization[2]	$4,260,000	$ 5,140,000	$ 4,650,000	$ 5,670,000	$ 87,800,000	$ 3,350,000
Total potential cash flow before bond amortization	$6,010,000	$ 9,640,000	$ 6,620,000	$ 6,160,000	$155,780,000	$ 5,350,000
Adjusted operating revenues	$9,440,000	$15,830,000	$15,970,000	$13,360,000	$296,100,000	$13,950,000
% of cash flow to adjusted operating revenues	63.7%	60.9%	41.5%	46.1%	52.6%	38.4%

1. For fiscal year ended June 30, 1971.
2. From Statistics for California Cities—1970–71.

SCHEDULE D-1

San Francisco Municipal Electric Facility
Comparison of Typical Electric Bills of Six of the Largest California Public Power Cities with Comparable Bills from Nearby Private Power Cities

	Santa Clara	Glendale	Anaheim	Pasadena	Los Angeles	Riverside
Residential 500 KWH	$ 8.39	$ 7.94	$ 9.35	11.70	$ 7.99	$ 8.93
Comparables	10.61(1)	11.09(2)	12.31(3)	11.90(4)	11.09(5)	11.90(6)
Difference	$ 2.22	$ 3.15	$ 2.96	$ .20	$ 3.10	$ 2.97
% to increase	26.5	39.7	31.7	1.7	38.8	33.3
Commercial (gen.) 6000 KWH	$ 125.55	$ 106.85(7)	$ 125.57	$ 122.00	$ 105.54	$ 117.47
Comparables	153.00(1)	135.13(2)	138.50(3)	137.37(4)	135.13(5)	137.37(6)
Difference	$ 27.45	$ 28.28	$ 12.93	$ 15.37	$ 29.59	$ 19.90
% to increase	21.9	26.5	10.3	12.6	28.0	16.9
Industrial (MUL) 100,000 KWH	$1,274.00	$1,022.00	$1,483.00	$1,530.00	$1,216.00	$1,407.00
Comparables	1,529.00(1)	1,489.00(2)	1,489.00(3)	1,489.00(4)	1,489.00(5)	1,489.00(6)
Difference	$ 255.00	$ 467.00	$ 6.00	($41.00)	$ 273.00	$ 82.00
% to increase	20.0	45.7	.4	(2.9)	22.5	5.8

Simple Average of
Percentage Increase
in Rate Needed to
Equal Nearby
Private Power City
Rates

| 22.8% | 39.7% | 14.1% | 3.8% | 29.8% | 18.7% |

Notes—

(1) Pacific Gas & Electric rate for San Mateo
(2) So. California Edison rate for Santa Monica
(3) So. California Edison rate for portion of Anaheim
(4) So. California Edison rate for Pomona
(5) So. California Edison rate for Long Beach
(6) So. California Edison rate for San Bernardino
(7) Average rate (no general commercial rate used)

It should also be noted that the 1970 national averages show the following costs per 100 KWH:

	Publicly Owned	*Privately Owned*
Residential	$1.47	$2.22
Commercial & Industrial	1.17	1.40

SCHEDULE D-2

San Francisco Municipal Electric Facility
Comparison of Local Property Tax Rates for Public Power and
Nearby Private Power Cities
Fiscal Year Ended June 30, 1971

	Public Power City	Private Power City
	Per $100 Assessed Value	
Alameda	$2.16	
Oakland		$2.80
Berkeley		3.275
Burbank	1.59	
Glendale	1.20	
Santa Monica		2.25
Los Angeles	2.57	
Long Beach		1.98
Pasadena	1.55	
Pomona		2.34
Anaheim	1.05	
Santa Ana		1.35
Riverside	1.13	
San Bernardino		1.75
Palo Alto	.74	
Santa Clara	1.42	
Menlo Park		.90
San Mateo		1.63

It should also be noted that the average California city tax rate for 1971–2 was $2.10 per $100 of assessed valuation. The average rate for public power cities in California for that year was $1.44.

Subsequent Events

SFNLAF expressed its "profound appreciation for the thoroughly professional report (API) prepared." It planned to release the report, and wanted API both to summarize it in language more "understandable to laymen not well versed in public utility or accounting terminology" and to answer certain crucial questions:

1. Is it economically and financially feasible for the City of San Francisco to acquire the electrical distribution systems of PG&E?
2. What is your best estimate of the figures (in Exhibit C) which most accurately reflect the cash flow after bond amortization for acquisition of PG&E's electrical distribution system, and therefore the financial impact on the City?

3. It is your opinion, based on projected revenues and expenses from the acquisition of PG&E, that the expenditure of money by the City for a feasibility study by a utility engineering consultant firm would be justified?

In a prompt answer which had been fully considered by the executive committee, API expressed its opinion, "subject to the assumptions and limitations indicated in our report of December 20, 1972, that it is financially feasible for the City and County of San Francisco to acquire the electrical distribution system of Pacific Gas and Electric Company located in San Francisco."

Since the amount of the bond issue required to do so is directly related to the present value of such facilities, and since such value can be accurately estimated only by appraisal and engineering studies beyond our competence, we are unable to estimate the total bond issue required. However, based on the data we have reviewed, we believe that the parameters indicated on Exhibit C of our December 20, 1972, report would adequately cover the final determined price assuming reasonably prompt action by the City on the acquisition. Thus the City would profit by between approximately $15 to $22 million annually by the acquisition of the distribution system alone, or by between $9 to $16 million annually by the acquisition of the distribution system and both Hunters Point and Potrero steam generating plants. Furthermore, after the bond issue is paid off (35 years), the City would profit by between approximately $29 to $33 million annually based on present price levels.

As a result of our findings, it is our opinion that expenditure by the City of the approximately $200,000 indicated for conducting a feasibility study by a utility engineering consulting firm would be warranted, since we understand such a study is legally necessary before acquisition action can be commenced.

As suggested in an earlier chapter, the term "financially feasible" is often confusing, misleading, and, therefore, misunderstood. API's letter did nothing to alleviate that difficulty. The intent was to demonstrate that, providing that the report's assumptions were accurate, the resulting cash flow would make it "financially feasible" for the city to acquire the distribution system. API did not recommend that the system be acquired; it stated merely that if actual operations approximated the estimates, the results would justify the acquisition.

The media did not recognize these nuances. Most reporters picked a figure to describe the projected "profits" (a term never used in the report) and ignored the parameters, assumptions, caveats, and qualifications.

The report apparently received closer and more careful scrutiny by the San Francisco civil grand jury. In a lengthy and thoughtful analysis, the grand jury released a report on the Hetch Hetchy Water and Power System in December 1973 as part of its annual review of city departments. In the heat of the national energy crisis, they noted that San Francisco had been confronted with its own energy crisis for many years— that of *disposing* of the cheap and environmentally clean hydroelectric power that it generates at its own powerhouses! The report focused on the history of the dilemma, the "questionable legality" of the current arrangements, and the resultant loss of "millions of dollars" of the taxpayers' money each year.

The report then traced the fascinating legislative, political, and legal history of the matter and the allegedly devious arrangements made to circumvent the Raker Act and various court decisions. It described the contracts between the city and the Turlock and Modesto Irrigation Districts, which it called "the great dumping ground for disposal of the city's power . . . ," and the contracts and tripartite contracts among the city, PG&E, and certain industrial users. It expressed concern that the violation of the Raker Act placed the city "in jeopardy of losing its Hetch Hetchy power rights."[2]

The report recommended the immediate leasing of the electrical distribution system and the necessary transmission lines from PG&E. It suggested that the annual rental be computed by applying the company-wide rate of return to the rate base for the facilities in question. The city was urged to evaluate, during the lease period, the assets it wished to acquire and to integrate these decisions with a recommended acceleration of the program to place the distribution system underground.

This innovative document was widely reported in the local press, but substantially ignored by city officials. Several weeks later, in an unusual move, the grand jury issued the following comments:

We have heard a lot of talk about the necessity of feasibility studies, enormous litigation, complicated legal affairs, et cetera. This is precisely why we recommend initial leasing of the facilities at Pacific Gas and Electric's rate base plus company-wide rate of return. This leasehold period will *BE* the feasibility study. If the experience indicates that it would not be economic for San Francisco to ultimately own the electrical distribution facility in the City, the lease can be terminated and PG&E and the City must then jointly petition Congress for an amendment to the Raker Act which would permit some of the existing arrangements to continue. However, since PG&E has not offered to abandon or sell this distribution system (as has been the practice of transportation utilities moving commuters) we must surmise that the electrical distribution system can hold its own and more than likely return a good profit, even after a more than generous purchase from PG&E. The Grand Jury's recommendations have

2. San Francisco acquired its own water distribution system in the early 1930s.

been met with the expected counterbluster of "years of litigation" and "financial impracticality" from sources who would normally be anticipated to oppose these recommendations. A much more constructive approach from this opposition would be a cards-on-the-table approach where the City would be given the complete facts as to the cost of the assets involved in the distribution system, its revenues, and the rate of return received, thereby enabling the City to determine the feasibility of the Grand Jury's recommendations without incurring costly consultant's fees. Many other companies have recently come to the conclusion that complete disclosure of their financial affairs can have a beneficial effect on their public image and we are sure that the PG&E, as a regulated public utility will soon determine that its best interests are served by making a complete voluntary disclosure to the P.U.C. of the details of its investment operation and profits in the City and County of San Francisco.

At about the same time a member of the staff of a local foundation informed SF API that an official of PG&E had complained to a member of the company's board of directors, who also served on the board of the foundation (which was then API's primary source of funds), that the API report was not accurate, fair, or professional. The PG&E board member appropriately referred the official to the staff of the foundation as the proper depository for complaints about a grantee. That meeting led to a series of conferences, summarized by parts of a letter that API sent to the foundation:

1. The Supervising Engineer, Economic and Statistics Department, Pacific Gas and Electric Company contended that the complexity of the subject was such that many disciplines were required to treat it properly. I heartily agreed and pointed out that we had had extensive discussions with attorneys, engineers, a municipal bond expert and an economist.

2. He indicated that his most serious overall concern was that "for API to submit a complicated report to a biased organization on a subject that requires many disciplines, without consulting PG&E on some aspects of the report is unprofessional." I heartily disagree. [He] himself was the PG&E official we contacted for certain information contained in the report which we could not obtain elsewhere. He was fully aware of our study but made no suggestion at that time that we review our report with him prior to its release . . . nor have we had any comments from them since its release, directly or indirectly, prior to [his] call to you late in November 1973. We did use every source we could find in an attempt to be objective and independent. The nature of the study was not one in which precision was possible or expected. The assumptions we used and the sources of the data were fully revealed. We believe that the figures in the report are supportable, and that our approach, our work and the report all reflect a high degree of professionalism.

3. [The supervising engineer] said that he felt we should have used more caution relative to the question of acquisition costs. We used a range of $100 to $200 million for acquisition of the distribution system. He estimated up to $600 million.

We used a wide range in an effort to emphasize that we were not attempting to estimate what the necessary bond issue would be. Only the PUC or the courts can determine acquisition costs, although an engineering feasibility study should be able to accurately estimate such costs.

Our range was developed based on a discussion with [the] general manager of Hetch Hetchy Water & Power Department. [He] estimated a $200 million acquisition cost for the distribution system and the Potrero steam generating plant based on an update of the latest feasibility report. Since that plant cost PG&E over $34 million and was originally built in 1931, we felt that the range of $100 to $200 million without the Potrero plant was reasonable and responsible. That conclusion was further supported in an overall way by reference to an interpolation of data developed during the recent controversy over the proposed municipalization of the Berkeley electrical distribution system.

In any event, the reader can easily expand our presentation on Exhibit C by $50 or $100 million increments. The effect of varying acquisition costs would not affect the cash flow before bond amortization. Thus this dispute would not relate to the period following the full payoff of the original bond issue.

4. [The supervising engineer] suggested that footnote 3 of Schedule A-1 (relating to the estimated wholesale price of electricity that PG&E would charge San Francisco to satisfy its needs beyond the capacity of the Hetch Hetchy system) was an "improper assumption because of a subsequent 22 percent wholesale rate increase." The rates we used were those available at the time and were those then in effect.

5. [He] expressed his conviction that the use of national averages to project certain expenses for San Francisco is a poor method because San Francisco wage rates are higher than national averages. He also maintained that City of San Francisco wage and fringe benefit rates are higher than those of PG&E for comparable jobs. Even if those representations are accepted, I feel the use of national averages was not only justified, but also conservative because of the high population density in San Francisco. The City . . . has 237 customers per mile of electrical distribution line as compared to PG&E's system-wide average of 35.4. The inherent economies in such expenses as service calls, transportation, meter-reading and others should, in my opinion, more than offset higher wage rates and result in lower unit costs. Only a careful analysis of PG&E's internal divisional reports are likely to definitively answer this question. It should be pointed out that the extremely detailed reports that PG&E is required to file annually with the PUC includes divisional breakdowns for revenue only—not for expenses. Thus, the use of averages would seem to have been the only reasonable approach for a study of this type.

6. [The supervising engineer] contended that our estimate of $500,000 for transmission costs was far too low. His estimate was $4 million. We used the actual cost of transmission in 1971 after consultation with an electrical engineer employed by Hetch Hetchy. We hope to give [him] the opportunity to substantiate his estimate.

7. [The supervising engineer] charged that plant replacements were not

provided for in our figures and that such costs would approximate $5 million annually. We used the term "capital additions" in footnote 4 of Schedule A-1. Perhaps "capital outlays" would have been more descriptive and accurate terminology. Such is the term used by the State Controller's office in its compilation of statistics for California Cities. Presumably it would cover all items of a capital nature. The historical amounts of such capital items related to the San Francisco electrical distribution system were not available to us. Thus the financing of them was assumed to be through bond issues (in the footnote).

Summary

We do not claim our report to be a feasibility study. We did attempt to analyze the available data and present it in an objective fashion to give our clients our opinion as to the advisability of pursuing the question of an engineering feasibility study . . .

We reaffirm our conviction as to the reasonableness, validity, and professionalism of this study. Should reliable information hereafter become available to us which would have a significant effect on the results of our study, we would modify our report accordingly.

The PG&E representative continued to disagree with the API report and to allege its misuse by "the people for whom (API) did the report and others." The foundation, however, was apparently satisfied with the response, for they continued their funding support.

In April 1974, two separate class-action lawsuits were filed, one in California Superior Court and one in U. S. District Court, alleging that the city's contract with PG&E for power distribution violated the Raker Act. The Superior Court action was removed to federal court on motion of the city, and came before the same judge to whom the federal suit was assigned. The federal suit relied heavily on the 1940 U. S. Supreme Court decision, which directed the city to cease disposing of electric power to PG&E. It further alleged that the subsequent contract between PG&E and the city differed only in form, not in substance, from the one struck down in 1940.

A committee of the Board of Supervisors of the City and County of San Francisco finally agreed to hold a public hearing in December 1974, to consider a recommendation calling for the authorization of the engineering feasibility study. SF API representatives were not invited to testify at the hearing, nor was the sponsoring supervisor present. The matter was not reported out by the committee to the full board.

Several months later, in April 1975, the federal District Court judge dismissed both lawsuits on the grounds that the plaintiffs did not have a private right of action under the Raker Act. The parties in the original District Court action have lodged an appeal in the Ninth Circuit. The original Superior Court suit was not appealed and has been dismissed.

Many policy lessons were learned in this case. The first is that there are dangers in using the term "financially feasible." Second, great care must be taken in dealing with the media on technical subjects. Reporters often lean on one figure or percentage to "describe" an issue. Frequently, the result is misinterpretation, confusion, or misleading impressions. One San Francisco semi-weekly paper ran a lengthy front page story about the controversy over the API figures that was distorted and inaccurate. Not only did the reporter fail to contact API prior to printing the story, but his paper refused to print API's letter to the editor in response to it.

Perhaps the most important lesson was the advisability of reviewing report drafts with all interested parties prior to final consideration by the executive committee and release. Although substantive changes were unlikely in this particular report, in several other cases such a procedure did prevent embarrassment.

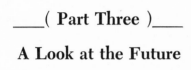

___(Part Three)___

A Look at the Future

___(11)___

Opportunities for Public Interest Accounting

How easy it is to develop traditions, even for an organization only a few years old. Perhaps it is especially easy for an organization of accountants, whose careers are based on care, caution, and conservatism, to fall into patterns of rigid behavior rationalized as traditions. Once established, those traditions are difficult to break no matter how slight their initial justification.

Yet the nature of the public interest accounting movement is such that tradition-breaking, far from being resisted, should be built into the organizational process, since the concept of the program itself has shattered many honored traditions of the profession. Gone now are the notions that only a program sponsored by the organized profession can be successful, that accountants deal only with direct services to clients rather than analyses of issues, and that they fully satisfy their social and community responsibilities by serving those who can afford to pay.

Still, many new "traditions" weigh heavily on the neophyte movement. Some say that Accountants for the Public Interest should not initiate their own cases or studies for fear of losing the reputation for objectivity that comes with having a "client." Others urge avoidance of competition with the rest of the profession, foregoing all compensation, performing only "issue-oriented" work, and the like.

The focus should remain on the needs and opportunities for service within our society that are not being met by the established profession. These needs will shift constantly and will differ from community to community. APIs must be structurally and philosophically flexible enough to meet them—if they can and if the needs are compatible with their purpose: to help make known all sides of public policy issues and to make the expertise of the accounting profession available to all segments of society.

Obviously, this is not to say that restrictions imposed by liability insurance policies, state licensing agencies, or the Internal Revenue Service may be taken lightly. Even here, the insurance policy perhaps can be endorsed to fit program modifications. Laws that never contemplated a pro bono accounting organization can be changed to accommodate this development, and IRS rulings often can be successfully challenged. Self-imposed constraints should be evaluated with at least equal aggressiveness. These are the attitudes to be encouraged if APIs are to become a vital force.

The corresponding danger is an overcommitment of available resources. The program of one of NAAPI's local affiliates still encompasses issue-oriented case work, internal accounting assistance to nonprofit organizations, assistance to minority business, and tax assistance to the poor. Such a broad program may be impossible to carry out. The wiser course seems to be to take on issues first. When that component is functioning effectively, other programs can be adopted.

Functions of the National Organization

The National Association of Accountants for the Public Interest is not the only vehicle through which the public interest accounting program could be conducted. It just happens to be the only game in town. It has also spread the movement, awakened the consciousness of professional accountants, and moved some of the leaders of the profession toward an appreciation of their social responsibilities.

By 1977, fourteen other local organizations had been formed as a direct result of the efforts and encouragement, first, of San Francisco Accountants for the Public Interest, and later of NAAPI. They are located in Portland (Oregon), Los Angeles, Philadelphia, Washington, New York, Newark, Chicago, Providence, Boston, Helena (Montana), Miami, Denver, Austin, and Atlanta. Several other groups are in the planning stages.

Two past presidents of the American Institute of Certified Public Accountants have joined the board of directors of NAAPI. Their willingness to lend their support has greatly enhanced the movement's respectability at the highest levels of the profession. Meetings have been held with all of the managing partners of the "Big Eight" national CPA firms and the president and chairman of the board of the AICPA. NAAPI representatives have been invited to speak to meetings of the Institute, the American Accounting Association, the National Association of Accountants, and several state CPA societies.

However, even more support is needed from the profession, and in particular the national firms, in the form of funds, moral encouragement, and volunteer participation. Few staff members or partners in local offices of national firms are brave enough to participate in a new and potentially controversial program without the approval of the head office. Only an organization with a national presence and a national constituency can function effectively in this milieu.

NAAPI also has served as a coordinator and information center. Case reports are available to others who are conducting or contemplating similar projects, and access to people with specialized knowledge or experience is provided. The bimonthly newsletter relates summaries of the significant activities of all the affiliates. NAAPI provides advice and documents regarding incorporation, tax exemption, foundation proposals, model engagement letters, and many other organizational and programmatic matters.

NAAPI also has raised funds for redistribution to affiliates to help them get started, and has assisted some in identifying and negotiating with local funding sources. It seeks long-range sources of funds to help local groups on a continuing basis.

The national organization must also develop the capacity to coordinate national cases. Problems of mass transit, health care, housing, utility regulations, public education, and a host of others cry out for accounting input. The public interest accounting movement can make its greatest contribution in the national arena.

Some Fertile Fields

There are many opportunities for expanding the services of a public interest accounting organization. Arbitration and mediation offer an interesting example. Those involved in this work regard objectivity with respect bordering on reverence. Both are frequently concerned with financial matters, and neither has so far significantly involved *the* profession that is educated and trained in this field and the only one generally recognized for its independence. Particularly when the dispute involves public policy or broad issues, such as the increasingly frequent public employee strikes, public interest accountants would be valuable participants in the search for solutions.

The judiciary frequently must make decisions on subjects with financial or economic significance. Occasionally, courts receive conflicting testimony on accounting matters by opposing expert witnesses. Few judges have accounting knowledge or training. Like them, their staff assistants and clerks usually have purely legal backgrounds. Within administrative and legal restrictions, society might gain much if the courts had analytical or interpretive accounting assistance from professionals who took no part in the formal proceedings.

Most legislators are also attorneys. Yet they are expected to comprehend the fiscal impact of their votes on an incredible range of issues. Some state legislatures have technical agencies to provide some of the missing information. Legislators in even the largest states, however, cannot get all the help they need. In several states, such agencies have themselves sought assistance in specialized fields beyond their competence. Several federal agencies have also approached APIs seeking independent opinions on proposed legislation or regulations, or on the implementation of existing laws and rulings. Within the constraints of present IRS restrictions on lobbying by tax exempt organizations, responding to these demonstrable needs appears to be not only an opportunity but a responsibility.

The grand jury system has been misused and discredited of late. In those states where they still exist, civil grand juries can serve as watchdogs on local government, but their performances could be greatly enhanced by the advice of professional accountants. The juries are, by definition, composed of laymen. They have almost no funds for staff help, and they are expected to evaluate the performance of huge, complex departments of government, to propose new laws, and to protest abuses—with no access to outside technical expertise.

Writing in the October 1974 issue of the *Progressive,* Marcus Raskin, codirector of the Institute for Policy Studies, recommended the establishment of a system of grand juries in each congressional district to redress the balance of power between the legislative and executive branches and to provide citizens with the means to participate more fully in the federal decision-making process. He sees such a system as a counterforce to the bureaucracy, the large corporations, and the military. Each grand jury would be authorized to investigate the institutions within its district, debate existing and proposed legislation, initiate issues for Congress to consider, point out abuses, and recommend program changes. Each would have a continuing mandate to facilitate full citizen participation through the establishment of such structures as local assemblies—in the New England town meeting tradition. Surely public interest accountants could play a major role in implementing this intriguing idea.

All fifteen local affiliates of NAAPI provide analyses of "issues." Some work on one or more of the other program components. A clearer understanding of the role that a local should play with respect to these other components would minimize certain problems associated with them. An API need only act as a broker, matching the demand for services (the clients for tax assistance, say) with the supply (the accountant volunteers). For the most part, neither knows how to reach the other now.

These direct services should include some type of screening procedure for both the suppliers, who should have demonstrable competence, and the clients, who should have reasonable needs and an inability to pay for the services. But, where it acts merely as a broker, the organization should not issue reports or treat the matter as its own project. A written understanding to that effect with the "client" of the volunteer would eliminate the need for supervision and review by the organization's staff or board and should minimize exposure to professional liability problems.

Another Look at Advocacy

The subject of advocacy has been treated early and often in the brief history of APIs and in the course of this book. Nonadvocacy has somehow been equated with independence, objectivity, and perhaps even honesty and integrity. APIs have taken great pains to declare and establish their status as nonadvocates. They felt that their credibility depended on it, and their history suggests that they have been nonadvocates in deed as well as word. Not even the friends of the movement—let alone the critics—have fully accepted the truth of that contention.

The view that advocacy should be avoided at all costs and that it is antithetical to objectivity has come under challenge. Advocacy is inseparable from the adversary process and is fundamental to America's political and economic system. In a public policy dispute involving government and industry or two branches of government, both parties openly and forcefully advocate their positions. Why shouldn't independent analysts examine the issue, decide on a course of action, and vigorously espouse it? If the arena happens to be a judicial or political one in which only one side can afford to pay for representation, assuredly the accounting experts on that side of the table will be advocating their client's cause, which is as it should be. Why, then, should the other side be denied such advocative support?

Advocacy is no novelty for accountants. Only in the performance of the attest function do members of the profession act as nonadvocates. In tax matters, the accountant is clearly and openly an advocate for his client. In management advisory services, he is paid to advocate the installation of systems, changes in product mix, personnel restructuring, and a host of other recommendations.

Objectivity is a frame of mind—of detachment or impersonality. In the context of an accountant's work, it should relate to the manner in which he conducts his work, his choice of documents to review, and the intellectual honesty with which he examines the results of his analysis. Objectivity need not prevent him from urging a policy or action he comes to believe in as information accumulates.

As discussed in Chapter 3, a public interest accounting organization might be less inhibited if it had no clients but instead initiated its own cases and studies. It would then represent no other group that might appear to taint its work. It would avoid problems of confidentiality and competition, and it would also avoid destroying the program of a client it represents, as happened in the open space case reported in Chapter 9.

A Multidisciplinary Approach

It should be abundantly clear by now that the most effective public interest organization would be one composed of professionals from a variety of disciplines. Attorneys, accountants, economists, engineers, scientists, and others should participate in considering public issues.

The first formal attempt to embody this concept was made by an organization in Washington called Professionals in the Public Interest. Started in 1974, the group lasted only one year. The logic of gathering a group of volunteers from a variety of disciplines is self-evident. Getting them all to put aside professional chauvinism for the good of the program presented more subtle questions: Which profession should play the starring role? Which would receive credit for a case? How can one profession supervise and integrate the work of several others? How can effective control be maintained when a small paid staff does not have expertise in each profession? Can the ethics of the various professions be meshed?

The organizers of this group had a brilliant vision, but it was considerably ahead of its time. A prerequisite to success was the presence of viable public interest organizations *within* each profession. At the time PIPI began operations, only the legal profession boasted a reasonably strong public interest component. Accountants, economists, and scientists were just beginning to implement their programs, and other professions had not yet started any.

Once such organizations exist, the next step should be a loose affiliation among them. Close cooperation on case work would encourage confidence in each other's abilities, and promote the beginnings of an umbrella public interest organization. Its program would respect the distinctions among professions by working through the auspices of each professional group. In other words, it would coordinate the work of the participant groups rather than recruit its own volunteers.

The anticipated result would be more effective treatment of complex public interest issues without jurisdictional disputes and interprofessional conflicts.

A Question of Survival

There is no magical guarantee that the public interest accounting movement will flourish. The road ahead is long and arduous. For one thing, the survival of public interest accounting cannot be considered apart from that of the rest of the public interest movement. The death of public interest accounting would have little direct effect on public interest law, but if public interest law foundered, public interest accounting would likely go under too.

The accomplishments of public interest law firms would fill many books the size of this one. Their role in the Watergate affair offers an intriguing example of the scope and effectiveness of their work. Public interest lawyer William Dobrovir gained first access to the now famous Nixon tapes through his milk fund lawsuit. Tax Analysts and Advocates initiated the questioning of the President's claimed tax deductions. In a suit brought by Public Citizen, a federal court ruled that the firing of Archibald Cox as Special Prosecutor was illegal. And the Tax Reform Research Group successfully sued to obtain the release from the IRS of the list of 99 "enemies."

Public interest law was not created in a vacuum. It evolved from the apparent breakdown in democratic institutions. In view of the domination by big business of the political process through huge, and frequently illegal, campaign contributions, the control of regulatory agencies by the regulated, and the indifference of government bureaucracies to concerns beyond their own preservation, the system seems to be coming apart. The result has been disillusionment, despair, and a loss of confidence in our institutions. If the public interest movement can give the average citizen hope for some voice at the decision-making tables along with the wealthy and the powerful, that indispensable confidence can be restored.

The irony is that the public interest movement is generally seen as extremely radical. Yet it represents the essence of conservatism, since it attempts to strengthen our institutions and make them more responsive to all of our citizens.

There are a few characteristics of the accounting profession that distinguish its prospects from those of public interest law. None is favorable. The accounting profession has none of the ethical canons and considerations that characterize the legal profession. Nor does it have the long tradition of helping the indigent. By its very nature, the accounting profession is conservative, and, therefore, it seems to attract conservative people—who have yet to perceive the innately conservative nature of the public interest movement. Finally, the structure of the profession, with its huge international firms employing a major percentage of practicing accountants, is not conducive to dynamic new concepts.

Long-Term Funding

Approximately a half million dollars was raised for public interest accounting in the first four years of its existence. Over 95 percent came from foundation grants. On a continuing basis the annual budget for the national organization and twenty local affiliates would probably total between $700,000 and $800,000. The value of volunteer services would represent several times that sum.

To put the figures into perspective, a CPA firm of twenty professionals could generate $800,000 in gross fees in a year. That amount is about 0.03 percent of the estimated annual fees of the "Big Eight" in a recent year. It is less than $6 a year for each of the nation's 150,000 CPAs. Raising those funds poses the biggest problem facing the movement today.

Foundations have supported the movement generously in its initial stages, but always with the clear understanding that other funding sources would have to be developed for the long run. Those sources are not plentiful, and they must be developed with a watchful eye: there is always the danger of losing program control in becoming dependent on a few large donors.

First among alternative sources of funds must be the accounting profession itself. The support must come from a broad cross section of individuals and firms—large and small. Without that support from within, it is unlikely that substantial funds can be raised elsewhere on a continuing basis.

Support from government appears to be a possibility. Legislation introduced in 1976 by Senators James Buckley of New York and Edward Kennedy of Massachusetts illustrate the bipartisan attraction and newly found respectability of the public interest movement. Buckley's proposal would permit the federal government to reimburse attorneys' fees and court costs (which could include accounting fees) on cases it loses. The Kennedy bill, cosponsored by Republican Senator Charles Mathias of Maryland and supported by the Ford administration, would amend the Administrative Procedures Act by authorizing all federal agencies to underwrite the cost of citizen participation through payment of fees for attorneys and expert witnesses, and other reasonable costs to eligible participants in any of its rulemaking, licensing, or adjudicatory proceedings.

The proposed "Science for Citizens" program of the National Science Foundation offers another possibility of funding for public interest groups. It would enable them to acquire technical expertise to participate more effectively in the resolution of public policy issues with scientific and technological aspects.

These possible funding sources could well be either long forgotten or well established before this book is published. They are mentioned merely as evidence of the growing recognition of public interest organizations and the contributions they have made.

The problem of potential loss of program control is compounded, in the case of federal funding, by the fragility of such support. Shifts in the political winds, budget crises, and the like make this source undependable in the long run.

Project funding from foundations or government agencies interested in a particular study could be significant. The growing complexities of the problems with which both governmental and private institutions are concerned should provide ample opportunities to an aggressive and innovative public interest group.

Another possibility is broad public support solicited through a direct mail program in the mode of Common Cause or Public Citizen. Such programs are usually accompanied by attempts to identify and solicit individuals who might make sizeable contributions.

The acceptance of fees from clients—probably at a substantial reduction from normal rates—should be considered only as a last resort because of the many serious problems it could generate. It could diminish the likelihood of significant support from the profession, which might object to the competition. It might also stir trouble with the IRS, which is already looking for reasons to "disexempt" public interest groups. It could limit the services available to groups that could afford nothing, eliminate the potential for studies initiated by APIs themselves, and even reduce the supply of volunteers. In all, the acceptance of fees is not a palatable solution.

Conclusion

The ultimate success for NAAPI and its local affiliates would be signalled by the waning of the need for them. If the AICPA were to adopt their programs, all public interest accounting groups could immediately close up shop and celebrate! Until that unlikely day, efforts must be intensified to involve increasing numbers of volunteers and members in the program.[1]

Accountants have an important role to play in restoring the public's confidence in its social institutions and in enabling the system to demonstrate its flexibility and adaptability in the face of the country's changing needs. Indeed, accountants are uniquely equipped for this role by virtue of their analytical skills and generally recognized and respected objectivity and independence.

1. One reason that day will be delayed is that under the profession's present structure, the Institute has little control over the programs and functions of the various state societies, where the programs would have to be operational. The most that can reasonably be expected from the Institute is moral encouragement, program endorsement, and modest financial support.

In recent years, the accounting literature has rung with exhortations from leaders of the profession to its members to take responsibility in society beyond performing the accounting process fairly and independently. A consensus is evolving that the individual accountant and the profession can no longer remain detached from society's concerns. The long-time executive director of the AICPA and eminent author, John Carey, perceptively wrote in 1965:

The responsibilities of the professional accounting societies are to guide their members in adapting to change, to give evidence of their concern for the public interest, and to carry out the processes of effective communication . . . If the deeds and words [of CPAs] demonstrate a consciousness of the profession's social obligation, and a genuine concern for the public interest, the CPAs of the 1980's will enjoy honors and rewards beyond the wildest dreams of their predecessors.[2]

Harvey Kapnick, the national managing partner of one of the "Big Eight" firms has said, "If accountants are to gain their rightful place in our free-enterprise society, we must recognize that we are accountable not to management, not to government regulations, not to the profession, but . . . to the public at large."[3]

Russell Palmer, also a national managing partner of a "Big Eight" firm put it this way: "The problem . . . is that the public does not always know what is in its interest. The solution, however, lies not in voices from on high telling the public what it ought to have. Rather the solution lies in improving the objective data upon which the public decides for itself what is in its interest."[4]

LeRoy Layton, a past president of the AICPA, who serves on NAAPI's board, wrote that there is a "new and expanded role society is demanding of us . . . to continue to increase our competence, our independence and our concern to find ways of measuring those things society values."[5]

At some point the rhetoric must be supported by action by the leaders of the profession lest it become the object of derision.

2. The CPA Plans for the Future, (New York: AICPA, 1965), pp. 406–7.
3. Harvey Kapnick, *In the Public Interest.* A series of addresses and articles on accounting and financial reporting. (Chicago: Arthur Andersen & Co., 1974), p. 49.
4. Russell E. Palmer, "The New Partnership: Accounting and the Public Interest", *Tempo*, 19, No. 1 (Touche Ross & Co., 1973), p. 10.
5. LeRoy Layton, "What is the New Role of the Profession in Our Society . . .", The Accounting Profession, (New York: AICPA, 1972), p. 18.

It is an obligation of both the large firms and the Institute—indeed, of the entire profession—to support any worthy public interest accounting organization. As interdependent members of an increasingly complex society, everyone relies on the specialized talents and services of many others. When reasonable and identifiable needs can be filled only by others, it is justifiable to expect those services to be available on a practical and acceptable basis.

Accountants' responsibilities, social and otherwise, are essentially to themselves. They need fulfillment in their work and a conviction of its value to society. In the final analysis, neither a professional organization nor an accounting firm exists other than through its members or staff. Organizations have no soul, no conscience, and no responsibilities of their own. These lie in the level of commitment, involvement, and participation of their members and staff.

In an address delivered in October 1912, Louis D. Brandeis applied three criteria to a profession:

> First, a profession is an occupation for which the necessary preliminary training is intellectual in character involving knowledge and to some extent learning, as distinguished from mere skill.
>
> Second, it is an occupation which is pursued largely for others and not merely for oneself.
>
> Third, it is an occupation in which the amount of financial return is not the accepted measure of success.

A 1956 study prepared for the AICPA listed seven characteristics of a profession; here are the last two:

> An acceptance of social responsibility inherent in an occupation endowed with public interest.
> An organization devoted to the advancement of the social obligation, as distinct from the economic interests, of the group.[7]

If accountancy is truly a profession, if it deserves the monopoly position bestowed by licensing authorities, if its members are to be more than aloof technicians, then it has an ethical responsibility to respond to the needs of the times by giving help to the community from which it earns its livelihood. Society needs that help today more than ever.

The analytical skills and objective posture of accountants are critical

---

6. Arthur Tourtellot, *The General Recognition of Accountancy as a Profession,* (New York: AICPA, 1956).

necessities in the solutions of many pressing problems. Accountants *can* play a significant role in strengthening and restoring confidence in our institutions. But no single organization or profession can possibly do it alone. It will take the combined and coordinated efforts of all elements of America's complex society to bring about the social, economic, and political changes necessary to make the system work. Given some courage, some leadership, and some vision, it is a job that can be done.

Index

ABA. *See* American Bar Association
ABAG forecasting model, 82–83
Accountability, 25
Accountancy
   attracting students to, 28–29
   ethics in, 34–36, 37, 38
   formal apparatus of, 29
   image of, 24
   liability in, 38–39
   as profession, 157
     problems of, 24–25
     responsibilities of, 157
Accountancy, public interest
   client and case selection, 31–32
   first national conference
   funding for, 30–31, 153–55
   malpractice and. *See* Malpractice
     insurance
   need for, 11, 19–22, 23–24, 25,
     149–51
     in bond resolutions disclosures,
      106
     for campaign spending
      regulations, 66, 67
     in Hill-Burton program, 51–52
     to restore public confidence,
      155–58
   nonadvocacy in. *See* Nonadvocacy
   success of, 148, 155
   See also names of accounting
     organizations
Accountants, retired, need useful
   work, 24
Accountants Committee on Urban
   Action, 25–26
Accountants for the Public Interest
   (APIs)
   board members' diversity in, 35
   as brokers, 150–51
   case initiation, 147, 151

   case selection, 31–32, 125
   as competition, 36–37
   confidentiality and, 38
   conflict of interest in, 37–38
   deadlines and, 72
   flexibility needed in, 147
   focus of, 147
   funding for, 153–55
   growth of, 40, 148
   liability and, 38–39, 147, 150–51
   media and, 144
   nonadvocacy in, 34–36
     challenged, 151
   problems of, 36–39, 72, 147, 148,
     150–51
   public interest concept and, 3–4
   success of, 155
   See also Accountancy, public
     interest; National Association
     of Accountants for the Public
     Interest; San Francisco
     Accountants for the Public
     Interest
Accounting Aid Societies (AAS), 17–
   18
   as prototype for API, 25
AICPA. *See* American Institute of
   Certified Public Accountants
Alameda, California
   power costs in, 129
   property tax rate in, 138
   See also Peralta Community
     College District
Alameda County Legal Aid Society
   in Hill-Burton case, 50
   in Peralta colleges case, 87–88
     evaluation letter from, 106
     report to, 89–105
Albany, California. *See* Peralta
     Community College District

American Accounting Association,
  recognized API, 148
American Bar Association (ABA)
  Code of Professional Responsibility,
    5, 6
  Fund for Public Education, 7
  legal aid by, 5–7
  public interest law and, 7, 8
American Civil Liberties Union, 6, 38
American Institute of Certified Public
    Accountants (AICPA)
  Accounting Aid Society funded by,
    18
  accounting defined by, ix
  ethics code, 23
  on forecasts, 77–78
  NAAPI recognized by, 148
  on need for public interest
    accountancy, 156
  power of, 29
  on professions, 157
  on public attitude toward CPAs, 24
  on social responsibility, 12
  support for APIs by, 30, 148, 155
  support needed from, 156–57
Anaheim, California
  potential cash flow with power rate
    increase, 135
  power costs in, 129, 136–37
  property tax rate in, 138
APIs. *See* Accountants for the Public
    Interest
Ardrey, Robert, 3
Arthur D. Little Company, 36
Atlanta, Georgia, API in, 148
Auditors, independence of, 34
Austin, Texas, API in, 148

Bad debts, Hill-Burton suit and, 47,
    50
Batchelder, Robert F., 103
Bay Area Rapid Transit (BART),
    airport expansion and, 78
Bechtel, Inc., 78
Berkeley, California
  power municipalization fight in,
    125
  property tax rate in, 138
  See also Peralta Community College
    District
Berkeley Learning Pavilion, 86
Beth Israel Hospital, 48–49

Black capitalism, accounting aid to,
    13–15
Bond resolutions, importance of
    disclosures about, 106
Boston, Massachusetts, API in, 148
Brandeis, Louis D., 157
Brugmann, Bruce, 19
Buckley, Senator James, 154
Burbank, California
  power costs in, 129
  property tax rate in, 138
Business, corruption in, 61–62
Business Aid Society, 18
Business and Professional People for
    the Public Interest, 8–9
Business Week, publicized API, 39

California
  care of dependent children in, 53–
    54, 55
  property tax differences in public
    and private power cities, 138
  required Environmental Impact
    Report for airport expansion,
    72
  state regulations and API, 27–28
California Department of Health,
    API testimony on Hill-Burton
    to, 51
California Juvenile Court, 53
California Public Utilities Commission
  API attended hearings of, 33
  power revenues reported to, 125
California Rural Legal Assistance, 8
California Society of Certified Public
    Accountants
  public interest work by, 13, 25–26
  San Francisco chapter asked to
    audit campaign books, 63
California State Employees
    Association, 20
California Teachers Association, 20
Campaign spending
  accountancy needed for, 11, 22, 66,
    67
  problem of, 61–62
  San Francisco regulations for, 62–
    65
    model forms for, 67–70
    problems of, 64–66
Carey, John, 156
Case selection, 31–32, 125

Census Bureau, population growth
  predictions by, 82–83
Center for Law and Social Policy, 8,
  49
Center for Study of Responsive Law, 8
Certified Public Accountants (CPAs)
  aided black businesses, 13–15
  API not competition for, 36–37
  API sought support of, 29–31
  charity by, 11–12
  public interest work by, 12–13, 15
    need for, 156–58
    problems of, 13–15, 16–17
  tax assistance by, 16–17
  See also American Institute of
    Certified Public Accountants
    (AICPA); State CPA societies
Charity, by accountants, 11–12
Charity allowances, 47, 51
Charlotte, North Carolina, Accounting
  Aid Society in, 18
Chicago, Illinois
  API in, 148
  public interest law in, 8–9
Children, delinquent, in San
  Francisco Youth Guidance
  Center, 53, 55
Children, dependent, care of, 53–54
  API studied, 54–55
    report, 55–59
  client evaluation letter, 58, 59
  improving, 59–60
Civil Aeronautics Board, 72
Cleveland, Ohio, public power in, 123
Client selection, 31–32, 125
Coalition of San Francisco
  Neighborhoods (CSFN), 62
  campaign spending and, 62–63
  enlisted API aid, 63
  report to, 66
Coleman Children and Youth
  Services, 58–59
Common Cause, 155
Community groups, accounting aid to,
  17, 18, 25, 26
Community Tax Aid, Inc. (CTA),
  15–16
Competition, 36–37
  case initiation avoids, 151
Confidentiality, 38, 151
Conflicts of interest, 37–38
Connecticut

Accounting Aid Society in, 18
  tax assistance in, 15
Connecticut CPA Society, 18
Construction projects, accurate cost
  estimation needed for, 19–20
Contributions, unrestricted, 47, 51
Controversiality, 125
Cook, et al. vs. Ochsner, et al., 44
Corruption, problem of, 61–62
Corte Madera, California, open space
  dispute in, 107–8
  API agreement to study, 108–11
  API report on, 111–20
    sources for, 119–20
  assumptions about, 111–13
  bond issue failed, 120
  evaluation letter about, 121
  projections about, 113–19
    additional tax burden, 116
    additional tax revenues, 116
    annual debt service, 115–16
    annual open space maintenance
      cost, 116
    annual property tax rates, 117–
      18, 119
    approach to, 113–15
    assessed valuation, 115
    description of, 115–19
    education costs, 116–17
Cost estimation, accountancy needed
  for, 19–20
CPAs. *See* Certified Public
  Accountants
Council for Public Interest Law, 7, 38
Courtesy allowances, 47
Courts, accountancy can aid, 149
Cox, Archibald, 153
CSFN. *See* Coalition of San
  Francisco Neighborhoods

Dankworth, Ed, 103
Deadlines, 72, 122
Dellums, Congressman Ronald, 105
Denver, Colorado, API in, 148
Department of HEW. *See* U.S.
  Department of Health,
  Education, and Welfare
Depreciation, 46, 51
Des Moines, Iowa, Accounting Aid
  society in, 17–18
  as prototype for API, 25

Detroit, Michigan, Accounting Aid
    Society in, 18
Dobrovir, William, 153
Drake University, Accounting Aid
    Society at, 17

Edna McConnell Clark Foundation, 7
Emeryville, California. *See* Peralta
    Community College District
Environmental Impact Report (EIR),
    for airport expansion, 72
    criticized by API, 75–80 *passim*
Estes, Ralph W., 17
Expenses, fixed and variable, 46–47,
    51, 93

Federal Aviation Administration, 72
Federal Power Commission, 126, 127
Feather River College
    annexed by Peralta, 87
    general purpose revenue,
        expenditures, and deficit for,
        100, 105
    monies spent for, 91, 92, 93
Financial feasibility, determining,
    139, 144
    under Hill-Burton Act, 43, 44–48,
        49, 51
Financial regulations, accountancy
    needed for, 21–22
Flint-Goodridge Hospital, 45, 47
Ford Foundation, 7
Forecasts, problems of, 77–78, 111
    in airport growth model, 81–83
    in open space plan, 111, 113–19
Foster care, temporary, 57, 59
Foster Grandparents Program, costs
    studied, 56, 59
Friends of the Earth, 85
Fryer, Thomas W., Jr., 103
Fund for Public Education, 7
Funding, 30–31, 153–55

Gallup poll, on accountancy's image,
    24
General Accounting Office (GAO),
    reviewed Hill-Burton program,
    51–52
General Motors, 18
Glendale, California
    potential cash flow with power rate
        increase, 135

power costs in, 129, 136–37
    property tax rate in, 138
Gold, Jeffrey, 15, 16
Goodman, Professor Bernard, 15
Government, as adversary, 8, 9
Grand juries, civil, public interest
    accounting and, 150

Hancock, Loni, 105
Hartford, Connecticut, Accounting
    Aid Society in, 18
Hartford, University of, tax assistance
    program at, 15
Health care financing, accountancy
    needed for, 11
Helena, Montana, API in, 148
Hetch Hetchy Water and Power
    System
    general manager estimated
        acquisition costs, 142
    grand jury report on, 140–41
    illegal sale of power from, 123, 124,
        140
    Raker Act authorized, 123
    San Francisco purchased city-owned
        power from, 127
HEW. *See* U.S. Department of
    Health, Education, and
    Welfare
Highway projects, accurate cost
    estimation needed for, 20
Hill-Burton Act
    accountancy needed for, 51, 52
    Alameda County case, 50
    and API recommendations for
        California regulations, 51
    financial feasibility under, 43, 44–
        48, 49, 51
    measuring costs of free care, 46–48,
        49–50, 51–52
    New York case, 48–49
    New Orleans case, 43–48
        contempt proceedings, 49–50
        provisions, 43, 44
Hornblower and Weeks-Hemphill,
    Noyes Incorporated, 122
Hospital Audit Guide, The, 47
Hospital Survey and Construction
    Act. *See* Hill-Burton Act

Illinois, CPAs aided black businesses
    in, 13

Incorporation, advantages of, 27
Internal Revenue Service
 and API aid to legislators, 150
 APIs and, 147, 148
 sued to release "enemies" list, 153
 tax assistance by, 16
 tax-exempt corporations and, 27,
  150
Internship programs, 17
Iowa, Accounting Aid Society in,
 17–18
Iowa CPA Society, 17, 18
Iskowitz, Gary, tax assistance
 program by, 15, 16

Journal of Accountancy
 on Accounting Aid Society, 17, 18
 on long-term projections, 77
 publicized API, 30, 39

Kapnick, Harvey, 156
Kelley, Ying Lee, 105
Kennedy, Senator Edward, 154

Labor disputes, accountancy needed
 for, 21
Laney College. *See* Peralta
 Community College District
Larkspur, California, in open space
 plan, 107
 effect of alternatives on, 115–19
 passim
Law, public interest, 7–10
 accomplishments of, 153
 and Hill-Burton compliance, 52
 private practice and, 9
 role in Watergate, 153
 See also Legal aid
Lawyers' Committee for Civil Rights
 Under the Law, 8, 38
Layton, LeRoy, 156
Legal aid, 5–7
 conflict of interest and, 38
 lessons of, 16
Legal service attorneys, inspired API,
 23
Legislators, public interest accounting
 and, 149–50
Levi, Edward H., 8
Liability. *See* Malpractice insurance

"Loaned-executive" program, 31
Long, Dr. Clement A., 103
Long Beach, California
 power rates in, 136–37
 property tax rate in, 138
Long-term projections. *See* Forecasts
Los Angeles, California
 API in, 148
 potential cash flow with power rate
  increase, 135
 power costs in, 129, 136–37
 property tax rate in, 138
 public power in, 123
 tax assistance program in, 15, 16
Los Angeles Times, publicized API,
 39
Louisiana, Hill-Burton suit and, 44
Low-income individuals, accounting
 assistance for, 16, 17, 18

Malpractice insurance
 for accountants, 38–39, 147
 medical, accountancy needed for,
  21
 minimizing liability, 150–51
 for public interest organizations, 39
Management advisory work, advocacy
 in, 34, 151
Marks, F. Raymond
 on OEO legal aid guidelines, 6–7
 on public interest law, 8*n*, 9*n*, 10
Marin Community College District,
 effect of open space
 alternatives on, 116, 117, 119
Marin Conservation League (MCL)
 enlisted API aid, 107, 108
 evaluation letter from, 121–22
 Northridge Open Space Plan, 107–
  8
 report to, 111–19
Marin County, open space dispute in,
 107–8
 effect of alternatives on, 115, 116
Marin General Hospital, effect of
 open space alternatives on, 116
Massachusetts, CPAs aided black
 businesses in, 13
Mathias, Senator Charles, 154
MDA Construction Cost Consultants,
 78
Media, dealing with, 144

Medical malpractice insurance,
    accountancy needed for, 21
Medicare/Medicaid, accountancy
    needed for, 21–22
Memphis, Tennessee, public power in,
    123
Menlo Park, California, property tax
    rate in, 138
Merritt College. *See* Peralta
    Community College District
Methodist Hospital, 45
MFY Legal Services, Inc., 48–49
Miami, Florida, API in, 148
Michigan, Accounting Aid Societies
    in, 18
Mill Valley, California, in open space
    plan, 107
    effect of alternatives on, 116, 117
Minnesota Accounting Aid Society, 18
Minority-owned businesses,
    accounting aid to, 13–15, 18
Missouri, CPAs aided black businesses
    in, 13
Modesto Irrigation District, San
    Francisco sold power to, 124,
    140
Mt. St. Joseph's Home, 57, 59
Mt. Tamalpais, 107

Nader, Ralph, 8, 23
National Alliance of Businessmen,
    accounting programs by, 14
National Association of Accountants
    charity program by, 14–15
    recognized NAAPI, 148
National Association of Accountants
    for the Public Interest
    (NAAPI)
    functions of, 40, 148–49
    funding aid by, 149
    funding for, 153–55
    information center, 149
    malpractice insurance, 39*n*
    national case coordination needed
        by, 149
    newsletter, 149
    organizational aid by, 149
    success of, 148, 155
    support from accounting profession
        for, 30, 148
National Association for the

Advancement of Colored
    People, 6
National Conference on Public
    Interest Accounting, 40
National Health and Environmental
    Law Program. *See* National
    Health Law Program
    (NHELP)
    as API client, 43, 45
    Marilyn Rose and, 43, 44
National Science Foundation, "Science
    for Citizens" program, 154
Nebraska, public power in, 123
Neubauer, John C., 17, 18
Newark, California, power substation
    in, 123
Newark, New Jersey, API in, 148
New Orleans, Louisiana, Hill-Burton
    suit in, 43–48
    contempt proceedings, 49–50
Newsweek, publicized API, 39
New York City
    API in, 148
    tax assistance program in, 15
New York State, CPAs aided black
    businesses in, 13
Nixon, Richard, 153
Nonadvocacy, 34–36, 151
    challenged, 151
    in Corte Madera study, 122
    in New York Hill-Burton case, 49
Nonprofit organizations, accounting
    aid for, 17, 18, 25, 26
North Carolina
    Accounting Aid Society in, 18
    Hill-Burton violation in, 43–44
North Carolina CPA Society, 18
North Peralta College
    abandoned, 86
    Associated Students fought for, 87,
        105–6
    monies allocated and spent for, 91,
        92, 93
    See also Peralta Community College
        District
Northridge Open Space Plan, 107–8

Oakland, California
    airport expansion possibilities, 75
    property tax rate in, 138
    See also Peralta Community College
        District

Office of Economic Opportunity
(OEO)
grant to Accounting Aid Society,
17–18
legal services, 7–8
OMBE. *See* U.S. Office of Minority
Business Enterprise
Open space, conflicting "public
interests" and, 4, 107
Outreach, problems of, 13–15, 16

Pacific Gas and Electric Company
(PG&E)
API report and, 139–41, 143–44
API response to, 141–43
assessed value of San Francisco
property, 127
bought Hetch Hetchy power, 123,
124
expenses of, 128–29
held data needed for public power
study, 125
influence of, 124–25
opposed public power, 123, 124–25
power costs, 1970, 129
power revenues from San Francisco,
1971, 125, 126
power supplied to San Francisco
and rate per hour, 127–28
rates compared to public power,
136–37
real rate of return, 126–27
taxes paid in San Francisco, 127
Palmer, Russell, 156
Palo Alto, California
power costs in, 129
property tax rate in, 138
Pasadena, California
potential cash flow with power rate
increase, 135
power costs in, 129, 136–37
property tax rate in, 138
Peat, Marwick, Mitchell and Co.
(PMM) Report, 72–74
API criticized, 74–83, 85
predictions updated, 85
Peralta Community College District
annexed Plumas district, 87
API report on, 89–105
assumptions underlying 1965 bond
requirements, 100

average daily attendance, 105
fixed costs and, 93
bond monies allocated and spent,
89–92
Feather River share, 92
North Peralta share, 92, 93
budget allocation procedure, 93
capital expenditures, 90–91
by school, 98
Feather River share, 92
North Peralta share, 92
cooperated in API field work, 88
described, 86–87
federal and state grant revenue,
101
fixed costs for schools, 93
funded by bonds, 86
general purpose expenditures per
A.D.A. by school, 99
general purpose revenue,
expenditures, and deficit for
Feather River College, 100,
105
lawsuit against, 105–6
permanent campus plans, 86
personnel interviewed, 102–3
plant funds
balance sheets, 94
statement of changes in, 95
notes about, 101, 103
sources of financial information for,
101–2
Philadelphia, Pennsylvania, API in,
148
Piedmont, California. *See* Peralta
Community College District
Plumas Unified School District, 87
Pomona, California
power rates in, 136–37
property tax rate in, 138
Portland, Oregon, API in, 148
Pound, Roscoe, 4
Powell, Alanson T., 103
Prison reform, accountancy needed
for, 11
Private power
method of comparing operating
results to public power, 125–26
property tax rates and, 126, 127,
138
rates compared to public, 127,
136–37

Private practice law, and public
    interest, 9
Professionals in the Public Interest,
    152
Professions, responsibilities of, 4–5,
    157
Progressive, The, grand jury proposal
    in, 150
Projections. *See* Forecasts
Providence, Rhode Island, API in,
    148
Public Citizen
    role in Watergate, 153
    solicits direct mail funding, 155
Public interest, concept of, 3–4, 107
Public interest accounting. *See*
        Accountancy, public interest;
        names of organizations
Public interest groups
    affiliations among recommended,
        152
    funding for, 154–55
    as innately conservative, 153
    need for, 152, 153
Public policy
    accountancy needed for, 23–24, 25,
        149
    advocacy in, 151
    service professions and, 4–5
Public power
    expenses of, 128–29
    extent of in U.S., 123
    method of comparing operating
        results to private power, 125–
        26
    potential cash flow with rate
        increase to private levels, 135
    property tax rates compared to
        private power cities, 126, 127,
        138
    rates compared to private, 127,
        136–37
    See also San Francisco, public
        power in

Quality control and review
    mechanism of, 33–34
    nonadvocacy and, 34, 35–36
Quincy, California, Feather River
    College in, 87

Raker Act, 123

    lawsuits under, 143
    San Francisco violated, 124, 140
Rapid transit, accurate cost estimation
    needed for, 20
Raskin, Marcus, proposes grand jury
    system, 150
Reagan, Governor Ronald, 20
Reed Union School District, 117
Rental factor, 58, 59
Reports, 33–34, 144
Retired accountants, need useful
    work, 24
Riverside, California
    potential cash flow with power rate
        increase, 135
    power costs in, 129, 136–37
    property tax rate in, 138
Rockefeller Brothers Fund, 7
Rose, Marilyn, Hill-Burton study and,
    43–45
    and contempt suit, 49
Rubard, Ray, 103

San Antonio, Texas, public power in,
    123
San Bernardino, California
    power rates in, 136–37
    property tax rate in, 138
San Francisco, California
    API began in, 23, 25–26
    accounting methods, 55
    campaign spending regulations in,
        62–63, 63–65
        problems of, 64–66
        model forms for, 67–70
    dependent child care in, 53–54
        API studied, 54–55
        report, 55–59
        improving, 59–60
    high-rise construction dispute,
        accountancy and, 19
    high-rise initiative, 62
    jurisdictional dispute with San
        Mateo County, 84, 85
    neighborhood politics in, 62
    PG&E property and taxes in, 127
    power revenues, 1971, 125, 126
    public interest law in, 8
    public power in
        acquisition of facilities for
            costs of, 126, 127, 141–42
        effect on city profits of, 127

financial feasibility of, 139
API report on, 126–38
aftermath of, 139–44
bond amortization for
projected annual cash flow
before and after, 125–26,
130–34
time period for, 127
civil grand jury report on, 139–41
data gathering about, 125–26
engineering feasibility study
about, 124
history of, 123–24
lawsuits about, 143
PG&E opposition to, 124–25,
141–43
San Francisco Accountants for the
Public Interest
in airport expansion case, 71–74
April '74 report, 81–83
client evaluation letters, 84
growth model scrutinized, 81–83
May '73 report, 74–77
October '73 report, 77–79, 81
outcome, 84–85
beginnings of, 23, 25–26
board of directors, 26–27
in campaign spending case, 63
on inadequacies of law, 63–66
model campaign spending report
system, 63, 67–70
report, 66
seminars held for campaign
treasurers, 66
client and case selection, 31–32, 125
client evaluation letters
Alameda County Legal Aid
Society, 106
finance director, Corte Madera,
121
Hornblower and Weeks-
Hemphill, Noyes Incorporated,
122
Marin Conservation League,
121–22
San Francisco Ecology Center, 84
Youth Law Center, 58, 59
as competition, 36
in dependent children case, 54–55
client evaluation letter, 58, 59
conclusion, 59–60
report, 56–58, 59

educational activities, 28–29
encouraged new chapters, 39–40
executive committee role, 32, 33
funding for, 30–31
gaining support for, 29–31
in Hill-Burton cases
Alameda County, 50
New Orleans, 43, 45–48
contempt proceedings, 49–50
New York, 48–49
testimony to California
Department of Health, 51
incorporated, 27
leadership of, 26–27
licensing regulations and, 28
methods, 31–34
nonadvocacy in, 18–19, 34–36
in open space case, 108
client evaluation letters, 121–22
outcome, 120
problems of, 120–21, 122
report, 111–19
sources of information for,
119–20
terms of, 108–11
organization, 26–29
in Peralta colleges case, 87–88
aided in lawsuit, 106
client evaluation letter, 106
field work described, 88
outcome, 105–6
report, 89–105
provisions for services, 31–32
in public power case, 123–25
acquisition costs, 126, 127, 141–
42
client evaluation letter, 138
data gathering, 125–26
financial feasibility of acquisition,
139
lessons of, 144
outcome, 143
report, 126–38
criticized, 141
defended, 141–43
quality control and review, 33–34
recurring problems in, 108
reports, about, 33–34, 144. *See also*
individual cases
scope of activities, 25–26
team approach used in, 32–34
terms of assistance, 31–32

uniqueness of cases, 32
volunteers in, 32, 33
recruiting, 28–29
San Francisco Airports Commission, 71, 72
San Francisco Bay Area, API and, 28–29
San Francisco Board of Supervisors, 72
San Francisco Department of Health, 57, 59
San Francisco Department of Social Services, 57, 59
San Francisco Ecology Center
in airport expansion case, 71–72, 77
evaluation letters from, 84
San Francisco Family Service Agency, 56
San Francisco Foundation
Coleman Project, 58, 59–60
dependent child care bequest, 54
San Francisco International Airport expansion
API aid enlisted for, 71–72
API reports on, 74–83
April '74, 81–83
May '73, 74–77
October '73, 77–79, 81
client evaluation letters, 84
current status of, 84–85
debated, 71
growth model scrutinized, 81–83
PMM report on, 72–74
updated, 85
population growth forecasts, 82–83
staging recommended for, 79–80
San Francisco Neighborhood Legal Assistance Foundation (SFNLAF), public power case, 124
enlisted API aid, 124
evaluation letter from, 138
questions on report, 138–39
answers to, 126–29
San Francisco Parent Teacher Association, 36
San Francisco Planning and Urban Renewal Association (SPUR), 19
San Francisco Planning Commission, 72

San Francisco Police Department, 57–58, 59
San Francisco Public Utilities Commission, 57, 59
San Francisco Tomorrow, 85
San Francisco Unified School District
API report prompted new CPA help, 36
education costs for dependent children, 56, 59
San Mateo, California
power rates in, 136–37
property tax rate in, 138
San Mateo County, in jurisdictional dispute, 84, 85
Santa Ana, California, property tax rate in, 138
Santa Clara, California
potential cash flow with power rate increase, 135
power costs in, 129, 136–37
property tax rate in, 138
Santa Monica, California
power rates in, 136–37
property tax rate in, 138
Sara Mayo Hospital, 45
School reform, accountancy needed for, 11
Seattle, Washington, public power in, 123
Shirck, Maudelle, 105
Sierra Club, 85
Sletteland, Greggar, 19
Small businesses, accounting aid to, 13–15, 17, 18
Smith, Chesterfield, 7
Smith, Reginald Heber, 6
Social welfare, conflicting "public interests" and, 4
Southern California Edison, rates compared to public power, 136–37
Stanford Research Institute, 36
State CPA societies
NAAPI recognized by, 148
tax assistance by, 16–17
See also individual states
State taxation and spending, accountancy needed for, 20–21

Stern Fund, funded API, 30
Storrer, Philip, 15, 16
Supreme Court, on public power for
  San Francisco, 124

Taft, Senator Robert, Hill-Burton Act
  and, 44
Tamalpais Union High School District,
  effect of open space plan on,
  115–19 *passim*
Tax accounting, advocacy in, 151
Tax Analysts and Advocates, role of
  in Watergate, 153
Tax assistance programs, 15–17
  by Accounting Aid Societies, 18
  outreach problems, 16
  vetoed by API, 26
Tax laws, corruption and, 61
Tax Reform Research Group, role of
  in Watergate, 153
Tourtellot, Arthur, 157*n*
Turlock Irrigation District, San
  Francisco power sold to, 124,
  140

Ultimate Highrise, The (Brugmann
  and Sletteland), 19
United Crusade, rejected funding
  request, 30
U.S. Commission on Civil Rights, 14
U.S. Department of Health,
  Education, and Welfare
  (HEW)
  API funding rejected by, 30
  funds Foster Grandparents
  Program, 56
  Hill-Burton compliance and, 43, 52
  North Carolina Hill-Burton
  violation and, 43–44

sued under Hill-Burton Act, 44
U.S. Office of Minority Business
  Enterprise (OMBE), 13, 14
U.S. Senate
  investigated Hill-Burton accounting,
  51
  testimony on Hill-Burton provisions,
  44
*United States vs. the City and County
  of San Francisco*, 124
United Way, 38
Urban Institute, recommended API,
  45
Urban League, accounting aid
  program by, 15
Utility regulations, accountancy
  needed for, 11

Volunteers
  in Accounting Aid Societies, 17, 18
  API use of, 32, 33
  liability and, 39
  recruiting, 28–29
  students as, 17, 18, 28–29, 32

Wall Street Journal, The, publicized
  API, 39
Washington, D.C.
  API in, 148
  public interest law in, 8
Widener, Mayor Warren, 105
W. J. Nicholson Co., 78

Yale Law Journal, on public interest
  law, 7
Youth Guidance Center, 53
  finances studied, 54–59 *passim*
Youth Law Center
  enlisted API help, 54
  evaluation letter, 58–59